B

ISBN: 979-8-9904484-0-7

This book is intended to provide accurate and authoritative information with regard to the subject matter covered. It is sold with the understanding that the publisher and author are not engaged in rendering legal, medical, or other professional advice. If expert assistance or counseling is needed, the services of a competent professional should be sought. In the event you use any of the information in this book for yourself, the author and the publisher assume no responsibility for your actions.

Printed in the United States of America

The

ULTIMATE
DOMAIN NAME
HANDBOOK

Your Essential Guide to
Buying, Branding & Selling
Great Domain Names

DAVID
CLEMENTS

www.brannans.com

FOR REBECCA:

Thank you for always being my steady anchor in a sea of ambitious, ever-evolving, and occasionally brilliant ideas. Thank you for supporting the good ones, gently nudging me to sink the bad ones, and still reminding me to take out the trash.

CONTENTS

WELCOME TO THE ULTIMATE DOMAIN NAME HANDBOOK

S OME WORDS IN the English language possess a sense of power apart from their meaning. "Domain" is such a word. Even the *sound* of the word conveys a profound sense of ownership, identity, and purpose.

A great domain name does the same—it establishes ownership, identity, and purpose.

At some point today, you've interacted with domain names—whether you've opened your email, bought a gift for a friend online, or seen an ad while going down the road. Domain names are so ubiquitous, most of us don't stop to think about them. Yet for almost two decades, domain names have taken up much of my thoughts and actions.

In his book *Outliers*, Malcolm Gladwell cites the "10,000 Hour Rule,"[1] referring to a famous study from psychology professor Anders Ericsson. To summarize, the rule says it takes 10,000 hours of intensive practice to become an expert in a skill.[2]

In the course of writing this book, I did some math and calculated that I've put in over 40,000 hours of time in the domain industry throughout my career.

Still, it sometimes feels strange to say I have "domain expertise," because it's such an ambiguous term. The time I've spent on the subject of domain names reminds me of one fact: I love what I do. I love helping people understand this complex, sometimes crazy industry, and I'm grateful it's how I get to spend my time.

And it's why I decided to write this book.

I've amassed so much knowledge of domain names, it feels wrong *not* to share it with others. Especially knowing firsthand the power and potential a great domain name has for you and your business.

People always have questions, but I realized no one else had ever put together a comprehensive and practical handbook providing the answers about domain names.

Have you ever wondered:
- **What makes a great domain name?**
- **How do you buy a domain name that's not for sale?**
- **What extension should you use for your domain name (i.e., .COM or .CO)?**
- **How do you find out who owns a registered domain name?**
- **How do you sell your premium domain name for top dollar?**

If so, this book is for you. It's the result of decades of practical experience, from consulting individuals, startup founders, and corporations on how to purchase high-value domain names that aren't for sale—to helping those same groups sell their high-value, premium domain names safely and for the most money possible.

If you're picking up this book, it may be because you fall into one of those camps. That is, you either want to buy a domain name—or you want to sell one. If that's the case, your individual purpose for wanting to buy or sell may vary, but this book is written specifically for you.

Domain names started out as a curiosity for me, but they have *become* my business—a business I accidentally landed in after a previous business of mine failed.

No one likes failure when it happens. Yet entrepreneurship has taught me how stories of failure are part of the learning process. It's also become an essential litmus test of honesty. If someone shares a story of failure with me, I feel I can trust them more than someone who approaches me with excessive bravado.

While I couldn't see it at the time, my business failure is what paved the way for me to learn about domain names. In the late '90s, I was part of a startup called MarTech with two business partners. Our product was disruptive technology at the time, designed to use cellular technology to track people and vehicles.

This isn't as "Big Brother" as it sounds. It was more about helping companies become more efficient and accurate with tracking their deliveries.

We did a corporate trial with a large, well-known home improvement retail company for their delivery vehicles. We also had another corporate trial with a well-known convenience store chain for their employees. In case of an attempted robbery, the employee could push the button on a pager-like device which would automatically alert authorities while simultaneously pinpointing the employee's location in the store.

Keep in mind, this was long before the days of the tech we all use every day, whether we need directions to a new restaurant or using "Find My Phone" to see where our loved ones are. Phones at this time were still just phones—they could call and send text messages and that's about it.

We had worked hard to bring this tech to market, but our big mistake was a lack of foresight for the oncoming digital transformation. Computers were still slow at the time and cellular was largely running on analog technology, not digital. Few people thought digital cellular would be the way of the future, so we ended up choosing analog technology, which meant we backed the wrong horse. Because, as it turned out, the horse was a dinosaur...

Looking back, it's easy to see that digital cellular networks would overtake the analog cellular network but in 1999 it wasn't as obvious to us. What we were using at the time is now referred to as 1G whereas 2G, 3G, 4G, and 5G are all *digital* cellular networks.[3]

While that was the most expensive mistake we made with MarTech, another mistake was with our domain name. Even though the internet was just starting to enter conversations when we launched in 1998, we had already named the company without giving a second thought to the domain name we'd registered for the website. It was less than an afterthought.

So when registering the domain name, I went with MarTechInc.com. Even by late '90s standards, this was a horrible domain name!

But you have to remember, there was no such thing as Search Engine Optimization (SEO) back then. When someone talked about branding, most people only thought of the logo and slogan. We had no idea what was coming in the world, let alone how to prepare for it!

On September 11, 2001, I found myself cleaning out the office because the business had failed. Meanwhile, the whole world was reeling from the terrorist attacks on New York and Washington. The uncertainty was palpable, in so many ways.

I remember one of my business partners at the time looked at me and asked, "What are you going to do next?"

It was a great question.

I'd graduated high school in 1986 with a 1.67 GPA. You pretty much have to *try* to get a GPA that low. My first attempt at college had been less than stellar, because I had never truly applied myself. Since childhood, the idea of becoming a doctor had bounced around my head. It was now or never.

"I'm going to go back to school," I answered. "I'm going to really apply myself this time, get good grades, and become a doctor."

Wanting a fresh start, I applied and was accepted to Kennesaw State University. I initially picked the Bachelor of Science Biology track, and in my first semester one of the classes I enrolled in was an introductory biology course covering cell and molecular biology, population genetics, and cellular anatomy and cellular metabolic processes in both plants and animals. I know—sounds exactly like the right background for someone to step into intellectual property and international business, right?

The biology professor, Bill Ensign—who became one of my favorite professors—surprised me by spending the entire first week of class talking about this new company called *Google*.

He predicted Google would change the way we researched information. He warned us about what kind of results we might find and showed us how to sift the information and identify whether a source was trustworthy or not.

Dr. Ensign's class would be my only B for the first three years back to university, yet this one lesson in Google forever changed my perspective about the possibilities of the internet. And after taking a beating from disruptive technology during the MarTech days, I didn't ever want to miss it again.

If you haven't guessed already, no, I'm not a doctor.

So what happened next?

A NEW DOMAIN

I had applied for med school. While I was waiting for the decision about whether I'd be accepted into med school, I was looking for something that would make a little money. One afternoon, at the suggestion of my brother Toby, I met up with an old friend of his, Rick

Latona. Over lunch, I asked him what he was up to.

"I'm buying and selling domain names," he replied. "I just sold one for $650,000."

My ears perked up. Simple domain name—a digital asset you couldn't hold in your hands—could be worth that much? I wasn't about to miss disruptive technology again. He had my complete attention.

After all, these were still the early days of the internet—where many people were calling it a "fad," and I even recall a news report when one anchor asked another, "What is an email address?"

Maybe it was similar back when Edison invented the light bulb— surely there were reporters who asked, "What does 'incandescent' mean?"

I'm a bit atypical in my love for spreadsheets and data. So in those early days when domain names had sparked my curiosity, I gave myself a creative exercise: "What kind of domain names might people want?"

Actual names were the first thing to come to mind. I was fortunate enough early on to buy DavidClements.com before some other David Clements could get it. But obviously, common names like David.com or Clements.com were already taken. Still, I added all these to a spreadsheet, filling cell by cell with ideas.

Scanning the room, inspiration hit: Every single *item* could have a .COM behind it. Desk.com, Lamp.com, Pen.com, Table.com, Sofa.com.

Another spark and I realized I could do the same by adding an "s" to the end of all these—Desks.com, Sofas.com, and so on. Every single word in the English language could attach a .COM behind it to become a digital asset. There was no limit! In fact, at one point, we even sold Sofas.com for over a hundred thousand dollars.

I began to see ".COM" behind everything around me and realized a new gold rush was about to happen. Anyone on the front end of it would stand to profit years later.

Within a year, I'd be in a formal partnership with Rick and Toby and for the next few years we worked together as business partners. We were buying and selling domain names, planning and running trade shows for those in the domain industry, and planning and executing domain auctions at those trade shows. I was working in the business full-time, putting in eighty to ninety hour weeks.

It was something like how the first car drivers must have felt. There were no rules of the road, no driving instructors—you learned by doing. So it was for me with domain names. When I sat to make a spreadsheet of potential high-value domain names, I came up with a list of 18,252 names. Oddly specific, right?

There are 676 combinations from AA.com to ZZ.com and 17,576 combinations from AAA.com to ZZZ.com. That's what happens when you like spreadsheets and data. Mind you, every one of these domain names was already registered. So, I'd look up the owner for each one and email them to see if they would sell me the name at a price I thought was less than the price I could sell the domain name for later.

Like in real estate, I was "flipping" domain names. Before long, I had talked to hundreds of domain name owners, bought the domain names, then turned around to sell them for a profit.

To put it another way, I was learning the business through hands-on experience only. I started out as a domain name investor, buying names cheap and then turning them around for profit. But then I came to realize I could monetize this knowledge and experience by being a broker.

My business partners and I embraced the brokerage model. We set out on the road to launch an international conference and a live domain auction company which took me to the Gold Coast in Australia, Amsterdam, Dublin, Milan, New York, Las Vegas, and Vancouver. I was the day-to-day managing partner—the "boots on the ground"—handling the negotiations with venues for the conference and with domain owners for the auction company. I enjoyed the work since it allowed me to interact with people.

It's surreal to think about those early days. We once rode bicycles from Atlanta all the way to New Orleans in February as part of a charity awareness event. We had failed to consider how this meant riding our bikes *into* the Westerlies all the way. It was cold as hell and several *very* motivated dogs chased us in Alabama, where apparently leash laws are optional. Still, we made it in the nick of time for the conference *and* Mardi Gras.

In many ways, the domain name industry can be viewed similarly to the real estate industry. While the value of a name can certainly go up and down, the long-term trajectory is one direction—*up*. The longer you hold onto a domain name, the more valuable it becomes. It should come as no surprise, then, that many mega-cap corporations will hold onto domain names they've acquired through mergers and acquisitions even though they're not actively using them. (But more on this idea later in Chapter 3.)

As a domain name broker, I help both individuals and companies with buying and selling premium domain names. Emphasis on the word *premium* because while there are over 367 million domain names in the world, we are really only interested in the twenty to thirty thousand which have significant value.

In 2010, I made the decision to go into business for myself and sold my interest in both the domain auction company and the trade show. Since Rick had started in the industry before me, we had done business under his name, so this meant I would need to do a total rebrand—which is where Brannans.com came from. You'll see why in Chapter 1.

Since starting Brannans, we've delivered over ten thousand premium domain names across seventy-five countries, including negotiations in twenty languages. My experiences have included helping brands acquire countless coveted domains, with many transactions going beyond the seven-figure mark.

More importantly, you can look at this book as the collection of what I've learned in those 40,000 hours. The years of learning and practice have culminated here to help you better understand domain names. My story may have started out with a failure—or failures, if you're keeping count—but it didn't end up there.

Every failure story can evolve into a success story if you're willing to learn and do better. One of the few good decisions I made in high school was to take a typing class—learning on an actual typewriter, mind you. Little did I know how much this would pay off later on during the Age of Information. My first failed stint at college taught me to take my work more seriously later on. And while I didn't become a doctor, I can credit Bill Ensign and that Principles of Biology course for opening my eyes to the potential of the internet.

HOW TO USE THIS BOOK

Like stock brokers, many domain name brokers develop the knack of buying low and then selling high. But unlike real estate or the stock market, there's no official oversight for the industry. In that way, it still feels a bit like the Wild West. It's not completely lawless, though—domain names are counted as intellectual property, so there are IP laws, international laws, and copyright laws which come into play, as we'll discuss later on.

Because of the lack of oversight, though, our industry largely happens behind a curtain of sorts. With this book, I want to pull back the curtain—and show you how it works, how "the sausage is made," so to speak. When you know what domain owners, investors, and brokers know, then you can select the best domain names for your own purposes and understand how to get the most value out of premium domain names.

If you're reading this, you belong to a fairly exclusive group of individuals:

Maybe you're a founder or an entrepreneur getting ready to launch a company, and you want to make sure you have a domain name that represents your brand while also boosting your online visibility. Great news—you'll find information here that will help you.

Maybe you're working for a Fortune 500, publicly-traded company and want to explore some options for safely selling a domain name that the company acquired from a merger or acquisition—you want to make sure to maximize the value of your asset but you also want to make sure that the money from any potential sale is clean, that you're not breaking any US federal laws by selling to an embargoed country or organization overseas. Great news—you'll find information here that will help you.

Or maybe you just inherited a domain name as part of a loved one's estate and you're not sure if it has any value or what to do with it. We have extensive experience with these delicate situations, and you will also find information here that will help you!

Whether you're here for work, or leisure, or because you're curious about domain names, I'm confident you'll learn something valuable you can use.

Since this is a handbook, it's not necessarily meant to be read from beginning to end. As such, there will be some repetition throughout as certain concepts and terms will apply to different topics. Feel free to skip to the section you're interested in and dig in. Or if you simply want to learn more about the domain name business, you can read from start to finish and treat any repetition as a review for yourself.

Part of what I love about this industry is how every domain name sale or purchase has a story behind it. These stories are the fabric of my experience, so I want to pass them on to you. Yet because every transaction is unique, I know this handbook can't answer all of your individual questions, so if you flip to the very end, you'll find links to some additional resources as well as an easy way to get in touch with our team for any further steps you need to take.

My greatest hope is you'll be able to view this book as a trusted guide you can turn to any time your thoughts cross paths with domain names. I want you to be able to easily get to the topic you're curious about, learn a concept in down-to-earth terms, and then go out and apply what you've learned.

Section I of this book will focus on **demystifying domain names**—understanding what they are, how they came to be, and understanding how the business works, including the major players in the industry.

Section II will focus on the role of **domain names as a marketing and branding tool**—including best practices for how to align your brand and company name with your domain name.

Section III will focus on the process of **buying a domain name**—whether you are registering one for a new company, or whether you wish to acquire an existing one from someone else. We'll cover topics such as doing your due diligence to avoid legal problems as well as knowing when and how to hire a domain broker or a domain attorney.

Section IV, we'll switch over to discussing **how to sell a premium domain name**—including determining if you have a premium domain name on your hands, the top marketplace(s) for selling, and cybersecurity risks companies should consider before they agree to sell their premium domain name. (Head's up—some names should *never* be sold.)

Finally, **Section V** will present you with a series of **case studies**, some from my own experience and some key industry examples. These will help you see how the various concepts throughout the book work together for a successful transaction.

At the back, you'll also find a glossary of terms you can consult as needed along with some additional resources.

Unlike many handbooks, this one will be packed with stories and real-life examples so you can see how these concepts apply to your situation. In the age where "content is king," you'll see why having a great domain name is not merely a functional asset, but one of the most valuable assets for your company. A premium domain name wields immense marketing and branding power, capable of establishing you as the go-to name in your industry. With the right domain name, you can drive traffic without excess spending on ads, increasing conversions for greater revenue.

When viewed through this lens, a great domain name truly has the power to help you take ownership of your brand, establish your identity, and even help you fulfill your purpose.

Your domain name is key in establishing trust with your prospects and achieving the hockey stick growth that you and your investors are building towards. *Words* have power. *Names* have power. Time to claim yours.

SECTION I

DEMYSTIFYING DOMAIN NAMES

CHAPTER 1

DOMAIN NAME GOLD

"During a gold rush, sell shovels."
–Unknown

SAMUEL BRANNAN LIVED a storied life, to say the least. Born in 1819 in what is now the state of Maine, he eventually ended up on the complete opposite end of the country where he became California's first millionaire.

At the age of fourteen, he ran away from home to escape an abusive father and moved in with his sister and brother-in-law in Ohio where he worked as a printer's apprentice, learning the basics of the news business. After his father's death, he inherited some money and bought some property outside of Cleveland.

Unfortunately, the land market crashed—and he found himself penniless. Soon after, both his mother and brother died from different illnesses—and the newspaper he worked for failed and closed up shop.

Eventually, he ended up in California and set up a store in Sutter's Fort (located in present-day Sacramento) and in San Francisco. Putting his printing experience to good use, he also founded the *California Star*, one of the first newspapers in the region. Then one day, in 1848, some laborers walked in and paid for their goods with gold. Not gold coins, mind you—but gold fresh out of the ground.

As you can imagine, this sparked his interest and he asked where the gold came from. "Sutter's Mill," they said. Then he followed the laborers out to the Sutter's Mill where he saw the gold with his own eyes.

What he did next was nothing short of genius. He went around and bought up all the shovels, picks, axes, and pans he could find in the area. It's reported he then ran through the streets of San Francisco, shouting out, "Gold! Gold! Gold on the American River!" Leveraging his newspaper, he published an article about the gold in the *California Star* to further spread the word. Sam Brannan literally started the Gold Rush.

A gold craze was sparked and everyone flocked into Sam Brannan's store to purchase shovels, pickaxes, and everything else they'd need to prospect for gold. The pans that Brannan had paid twenty cents apiece for each sold at a markup of *fifteen dollars*. Simple supply and demand. Within a few months, he had made $36,000—a gargantuan sum at the time.

When I discovered the potential of domain names, I felt like Samual Brannan probably did when he saw the gold. The internet was a new gold rush—and domain names would be the assets everyone was scrambling for.[4]

In today's world, domain names are unavoidable. You use them every single day, whether you own one or not. They make up integral parts of our work and lives. Maybe you've shared a photo on social media from your latest vacation, made a mobile order for the office, or just applied for the loan on a home—you've used a domain name.

And yet most of us go about our lives, not giving these pieces of digital real estate much thought—until you need to buy one or sell one.

Chances are, one of these scenarios will happen for you:

Maybe you're launching a new business and you're building your brand strategy.

Maybe you're managing a loved one's estate and discovered they have had the same domain name registered since 1993 and that it's worth six or seven-figures.

Two decades of being at the forefront of the domain name industry has given me golden experience in knowing a great domain name from a lousy one. After all, there are more registered domain names in the world (367 million) than there are words in the English language (170,000). Only around twenty- to thirty-thousand of these are what can be designated as premium domain names, meaning they can be valued at six-figures or more.

When I decided to hang out my own shingle and become an independent domain name broker, I had to do what many an entrepreneur has had to do—name my business and establish a brand. It was no question for me. Inspired by Samuel Brannan's story, the name of the company *had* to be Brannans. There was just one problem:

Someone else already owned the domain name.

Thankfully, I was able to buy Brannans.com from the previous owner—a story I'll save for later in the book. But this is the dilemma faced by many founders:

How do you choose a great brand name? And if it's a great brand name, chances are 100 percent that the domain name will be unavailable for registration and you'll have to buy it from someone—but how do you get it?

How do you know if the domain name you want to sell is worth a premium investment? How do you make sure the name isn't stolen? Or that it isn't infringing on someone's trademark? That you'll be protected—that you'll get the domain name and the owner will get the money if you do come to an agreement on price?

Before we can answer those questions, we first need to understand what a domain name is. It's on this foundation you can begin to understand which domain names are pure gold—and which ones are pyrite. You'd be amazed how many companies and people are out there trying hard to sell you Fool's Gold—and how much money they make from unsuspecting buyers.

DOMAIN NAME BASICS

To start with, you could think of a domain name as a digital storefront. Because it's digital, though, you don't face the geographic restrictions of a typical brick-and-mortar building. Imagine the great Roman Colosseum—there are many doors leading into it. But your domain name is the *primary* door leading to your business online.

Even though they are digital, domain names have an anatomy. But I promise it's easier than learning terms and systems from the anatomy and physiology course I took. Since you'll see these terms and acronyms used throughout the book, feel free to put a sticky note here for easy reference later on.

TOP-LEVEL DOMAINS (TLDS)

This can be confusing for those of us who read left-to-right, because the Top-Level Domain is the part of the domain name at the very *end* of the address. Put another way, it's generally everything to the right of the dot. Each TLD is also shorthand for a longer word representing the domain's purpose.

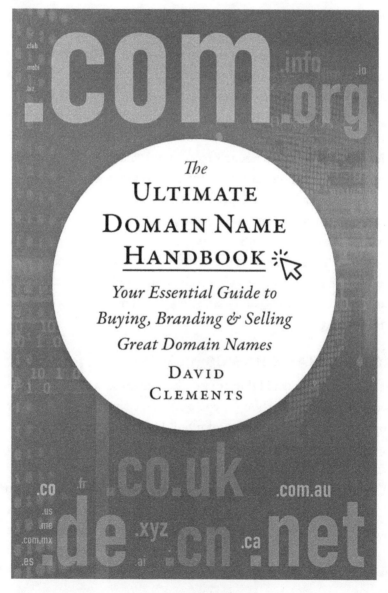

Some of the most common:

.COM = Commercial—used by commercial, for-profit enterprises.
.NET = Network—the original TLD, referring to an internal comput-
er-based communication network.
.ORG = Organization—typically a non-profit organization.

You'll also sometimes see these referred to as gTLDs, meaning Generic
Top-Level Domains because they are the most popular and recognizable
extensions on the market. Companies that sell domain names (such as
GoDaddy) are known as registrars, and most registrars don't sell *all* of the
available TLDs. Instead, registrars often focus on selling a few dozen or a
few hundred of the more valuable ones (i.e., .COM and .ORG names) and
dismiss the rest. From my experience, there are around 500 TLDs that
are globally relevant in today's market, though there are over 1,500 at the
time of writing this book.

I'm really happy with the way the book jacket design turned out. I
came up with the concept for it a few years ago to let people visually
see how relevant (or irrelevant) alternative TLDs were. Ultimately, we
decided to go with 22 TLDs on the cover. Of course, the .COM is the largest – but most of the TLDs on the cover are proportional to the number
of registrations each one has. The obvious exception to this is the .COM
– it would need to be much larger but that wouldn't fit on the page and it
didn't look right. I finally settled on the size it is now, and most of the rest
of the TLDs are proportional to their registration numbers. Most people
don't notice .TEL at first. It's the smallest of the bunch and barely legible
because it's so small. It's located above the "." in .CN.

There are many other alternative TLDs, of course, such as .CO, .MOBI,
.ME, .BIZ, .INFO, .XYZ, and the infamous .XXX. New ones are emerging or
gaining popularity even as this book was being developed, such as the
boom of .AI and .APP. Time will tell whether the popularity of these will
stick, but if history is any indicator, we're likely looking at the "flavor of
the month," not a change in consumer behavior. More often than not,
these newer TLDs turn out to be pyrite.

To this day, though, if you think of it like real estate, .COM is still *the* prime property—the gold when it comes to TLDs. And with a few ccTLDs as exceptions, everything else falls into the pyrite category. Statistically relevant data proves this at a high confidence interval. All you have to do is look at a list of domains Fortune 500 companies are using or a list of the most expensive domain names sold. Over 95 percent are .COMs (see Chapter 3).

You'll also likely recognize what are sometimes called sTLDs (Sponsored Top-Level Domains), which have restrictions on who can register them.

These include:

.GOV = Government—used by government agencies at all levels.
.EDU = Education—typically used by universities and other institutions of higher learning.
.MIL = Military—used by branches of the military, particularly in the US.

As you can imagine, it would be chaos if *anyone* could register a .GOV or .MIL domain name, which is why these are designated as "sponsored" TLDs. You wouldn't want a scammer, terrorist, or cybercriminal registering these addresses and wreaking havoc on people's lives!

COUNTRY CODE TOP-LEVEL DOMAINS (CCTLDS)

If you've ever had to make an international phone call, then you know that each country in the world has its own country code which must be dialed before the rest of the number. Likewise, there are over 300 country code TLDs. If you're curious why there are more ccTLDs than there are nations, it's because some *regions* have their own ccTLDs, such as Puerto Rico, which is a US territory.

Some examples:

.US = United States
.PR = Puerto Rico
.ES = Spain

.FR = France
.DE = Germany
.IT = Italy
.IN = India
.CO.UK = United Kingdom[5]

Where this can sometimes become confusing is that some ccTLDs cross over with gTLDs, such as .ME which is the country code for the nation of Montenegro but which also become popular for use in personal branding. It's also been used by some companies when expanding into the Middle East as a way for them to signal they're targeting the entire region rather than any particular country. Likewise, .CO is the ccTLD for the nation of Colombia, but has also been used as a shorthand for "Company."

To help keep all of this straight, you may have heard of **ICANN—Internet Corporation for Assigned Names and Numbers**. Established in 1998, they are a nonprofit, international partnership based in Los Angeles and according to their own website:

"[ICANN] promotes competition and develops policy on the Internet's unique identifiers."[6]

As such, they are involved in the regulation of what TLDs may be used, how registries can use them, and rules regarding the release of new TLDs.

SECOND-LEVEL DOMAIN (SLD)

As you've probably already figured out, the SLD (Second-Level Domain) is the part of the domain name on the left side of the dot dividing it from the TLD. More often than not, it's the name of the business or organization itself. For example:

- GOOGLE.com
- AMAZON.com
- KENNESAW.edu
- FBI.gov
- SCAN.com
- BRANNANS.com

No doubt, you get the point. It's here with the SLDs where business owners can exercise some creativity, but where they also have to give considerable thought and care to select a domain name that will boost their brand and marketing efforts, not bury them. As I mentioned before, I learned this lesson the hard way with the awful SLD we chose for MarTech (rest in peace). You can also choose an awful TLD, too. We'll be getting into criteria for selecting the best SLDs and TLDs in later chapters.

It's important to mention here that TLDs and SLDs are *not* the same as SEO (Search Engine Optimization), though they can play a role in boosting your website's SEO. We'll discuss this more in Section III when we get into how domain names can be used as branding and marketing tools.

In the next chapter, we'll delve more into the history of where domain names came from and how people started acquiring them compared to how it works today.

DEBUNKING DOMAIN NAME MYTHS

Over the course of my career in domain names, the same myths keep popping up. Before we go any further, let's go ahead and debunk some of these myths so that you can be set up for success, whether you're looking to buy or sell a domain name.

MYTH #1: KEYWORD DOMAINS WILL LET YOU HACK GOOGLE'S ALGORITHM AND RANK ON THE FRONT PAGE.

Once upon a time, you could throw up a couple of paragraphs chockfull of keywords on a basic website and rank well on Google. Back then, people were hacking Google's algorithm with keyword-based domain names to make sure they were getting on Google's front page.

For instance, if they ran a bakery in Atlanta, Georgia, they might register a domain name like BestBakeryAtlanta.com to try to make sure people would find them first.

Google figured out this trick and did some algorithm corrections with their Panda (2011) and Penguin (2012) updates. Unfortunately, this myth persists and people still think they can hack the system. They end up investing in domain names which are lower value and actually hurting their brand value.

The *only* legitimate, long-term way a keyword domain name is going to rank after the Panda and Penguin updates is for the website to be developed *and* for the content to be unique and relevant. Even then, that's no guarantee of ranking highly but you certainly won't rank quickly just because you have a keyword domain name.

Also, because of these two updates, keyword domain names don't have the punch they once did, so they aren't selling for as much money as they used to.

MYTH #2: MAYBE THE OWNER OF THE PREMIUM DOMAIN NAME DOESN'T KNOW HOW MUCH IT'S WORTH.

I'm frequently approached by individuals who say they want to buy a premium domain name yet end up suggesting a ridiculously low offer. Often, these individuals are naively hoping the current owner/registrant doesn't realize what they have on their hands. If you find yourself in this position, I'm sorry to burst your bubble—but I'm telling you now, they *absolutely* know how much it's worth. Guaranteed, a hundred percent. Why?

Most premium domain names were registered in the 1990s, so if the owner you're approaching has been renewing the registration ever since then—and they didn't sell during the Dotcom Bust of 2000—and they didn't sell during the market crash of 2008—and they didn't sell during the 2020—2021 pandemic and inflation spike—they're not likely to let it go for a song now. Keep in mind, this same owner also didn't sell during the boom times when they were receiving high-dollar, unsolicited offers. And they often have a broker like myself working with them already to at least appraise the name's value, even if they're not ready to sell yet.

Based on experience, it's a guarantee that some of these domain name owners have been getting offers of at least $50,000, and in some cases, more than $500,000 from speculators in the industry. This doesn't include the serious, legitimate offers that major corporations have likely offered on some of these domain names as well. Domain names are an asset class just like real estate and stocks—and the data supports they are more stable than stocks. Simply put, the longer someone holds onto a premium name, the more it's worth.

MYTH #3: ALTERNATIVE TLDS ARE JUST AS GOOD AS .COM.

Sorry, but they're not. And they never will be. For multiple reasons, too. You can't change decades of consumer and business behavior, and you can see some of the data in the Overstock example you'll see in Myth #5.

Even back in the early days when we were doing domain name auctions, the alternative TLDs like .TEL, .MOBI, .BIZ, and .INFO turned out to be duds. While these were popular in their time and everyone was talking about them when they came out, they're worthless now. I've gotten hate for saying so in the past, but the data supports my hypothesis.

In fact, the only two groups who consistently made money off of these alternative TLDs were the registries hawking them and the registrars selling them. I know of one domain investor who lost half a million investing in .MOBI, thinking it would be the next premium TLD. Every now and then an alternative TLD breaks the mold, but they are the exception, not the rule. The safer bet is going with .COM.

Generally speaking, you'll find only three groups of people who make money from alternative TLDs—the registries, the registrars, and the investors who flip them while they can. Sometimes the same person and/ or entity represents more than one of these three groups at the same time. We'll talk about these specific groups in Chapter 3.

MYTH #4: WE DON'T NEED .COM FOR OUR BRAND RIGHT NOW.

Phrased another way, this myth sometimes sounds like, "The .COM isn't worth that much to us," or even, "Let's just see if the current owners drop it when the registration expires, and then we can pick it up cheap."

Unfortunately, if you think someone has held onto a .COM for twenty-nine years and will just drop it in six months, you're living in a fantasy. This is particularly true if it's a generic, one-word domain like Batteries. com (a domain name I happen to own as I'm writing this).

One go-to publicly discoverable example is Ice.com. They were already a $40 billion company before they were able to acquire their premium domain name. Beforehand, they were using TheIce.com.

When the previous owner of the domain was selling their business, they discovered their domain name was the most valuable asset they had. They decided to separate the domain name from the business itself so they could sell it independently. Within hours of making the domain name available, they had multiple offers on the table.

In other words, it's never too late to upgrade to a better name—but you need to be prepared to compete and pay for it. One of many areas where having a broker can give you the competitive advantage!

Bottom line here: you can't look at a .COM domain like other expenses because it's an *investment*. On the books, you'll label it as an *indefinite lived, intangible asset*. In today's online world, it's the single most important asset your business has. That's no exaggeration. If you're in business, then you're online—and since you're online, you use a domain name. A higher quality, exact match, .COM domain name for your brand increases trust in your brand, increases traffic to your website, and will increase conversion rate on your site, too.

MYTH: #5: I DON'T CARE ABOUT HAVING A .COM. OUR BRAND WILL BE FINE WITHOUT IT.

Whenever this myth comes up, my first response is, "You *should* care." If you're launching a business, you want the exact brand match—and you want a .COM, period. Some think they can get away with .CO instead, but most of the time, people will still end up typing .COM when they go to their browser. Ignore this and you're essentially giving away your potential web traffic to another company.

One of the most famous failures around this myth was when Overstock tried to rebrand as "O.co" since "O.com" wasn't available. They thought since they had an established brand, the shorter domain name would be better for customers.

So they spent *millions* rebranding from Overstock.com to O.co. They shouted to the world, "Come see our store at O.co!" But guess what happened? Most people typed in O.*com* instead. In fact, according to reports at the time, when Overstock did the rebrand to O.co, they lost a staggering 61 percent of their traffic to O.com.[7]

What they didn't count on is how incredibly difficult it is to alter customer behavior. Eventually, the company had to revert *back* to the old domain name, Overstock.com.

One time, I witnessed a brand *finally* convert to a .COM domain name (Honeymoons.com) and saw their sales conversion rate increase seven times. You can see the full story in Chapter 10.

Moral of the story: I strongly recommend doing whatever it takes to get the .COM for your brand. The value of the .COM is why about 70 percent of our work is focused on acquisitions.[8] More on this topic in **Section III, Buying a Domain Name.**

MYTH #6: YOU DON'T ACTUALLY OWN THE DOMAIN NAME.

This might be one of the least talked about, but one of the most essential for understanding the industry. So far, I've used the word "owner" with domain names as a matter of practicality. But the fact of the matter is that you're the *registrant*, that is, the owner of the registration—and this ownership *can* expire or be transferred.

Being the registrant is a little like building on leased land. In 1598, William Shakespeare and famous actor Richard Burbage ran into a problem. They co-owned the playhouse cleverly named "The Theatre," but they had built it on leased land owned by Giles Alleyn. When Alleyn refused to renew the land lease, he claimed the theater itself belonged to him too since it had been built on his land. So what did Shakespeare and Co. do?

In the middle of the night on December 28, 1598, they took apart the entire building and moved it to new land across the Thames in Southwark, rechristening it as the Globe Theatre. Thankfully, in the world of domain names, we don't have to be quite as drastic.

While the registry always owns the domain name, you're paying them for the right to use it, which is why you have to renew the registration every year. Otherwise, someone else can swoop in and take it from you.

So while we're on the topic—it's a great best practice to make sure you have it set to auto-renew!

For example, Verisign is the behemoth in the industry because they own .COM. According to 2022 data, their revenue was $1.42 billion—mostly driven by domain name registrations. Whenever ICANN announces the creation of a new registry, it is typically followed by a bidding war—everyone wants to be the next registry owner because then *they* will own all the domain names.

One recent example was when .CLUB became available on January 12, 2012. CLUB Domains LLC filed their application with ICANN immediately. As various celebrities and associations began to register .CLUB domains for their fan clubs, the value shot up. Eventually, GoDaddy Registry acquired CLUB Domains LLC to the tune of $80 million according to SEC filings.[9]

In other words, "There's gold in them thar hills."

COMMON INDICATORS FOR PREMIUM DOMAIN NAMES

The question is: How do you know what's gold?

Over the years, I've established a few rules for myself to gauge whether a domain name is truly premium or not. While we'll discuss this further in **Section III**, it's essential to know the basics of what makes a domain name valuable. Whether you want to buy *or* sell, the same basic tests apply.

1. **Was the domain name registered before the year 2000?** If so, it stands a higher chance of being high value. It's simply the time principle like in real estate—prime property accrues additional value over time.

2. **Is it a one-word .COM?** Batteries. Amazon. Apple. Ring. Scan. One-word .COMs are *the* most valuable in the market. Sometimes a two-word domain name can be premium, but it's more the exception to the rule. One-word is still the best litmus test, so long as they are easy to spell, of course—which gets us into the next test...

3. **Can a third-grader spell it?** For instance, you can't assume any one-word is valuable simply because it's one word. Let's look at Onomatopoeia.com. A word like *onomatopoeia* is great for a spelling bee, but that's about it. Moo.com would be much better. If people can't spell it easily and quickly, it's not worth as much. And if a first grader can spell it, then the name might be worth even *more!*

If a domain name comes across my radar and it passes these three tests, then it's typically worth pursuing. I get calls every week from people who believe they have a premium domain name but it falls short on one or more of these common indicators.

For instance, part of Brannan's brokerage business includes helping families sell a domain name they either no longer use or need. Sometimes, it's a domain name they've inherited and they discover its high value. Often, the story is the same—their parents or grandparents acquired the domain name in the '90s, used it for a family site or a business, but now they no longer need it.

Just imagine for a moment what such a first name or surname-based domain could be worth. For example, Tom.com sold for $2.5 million back in 1999.[105] What do you think it would be worth *today*? (Clue: Rocket.com sold for $14 million in October, 2024.)[11]

What I've found is that families have often held onto these domain names, not because they could foresee a huge profit in the future, but because there is an emotional attachment. It represents their family or a business they worked hard to build. It holds true meaning for their identity. How do you put a price on *that*?

We'll get more into the branding concepts in **Section II** when we discuss the intersection of branding, marketing, your business name, and your domain name. For now, though, you can use these same tests to determine whether you are looking at gold—or not.

Before sharing about the players in the domain name industry, we need to take a slight detour to discuss the history of domain names—where they came from, how they've evolved, and how it's led to where we are today.

CHAPTER 2

A BRIEF HISTORY OF DOMAIN NAMES

HISTORY MIGHT FEEL like a strange word to apply to domain names, but seeing as how the original iPhone can now be viewed at the Smithsonian, it feels appropriate. To do so, we're going to jump in our DeLorean to head back to the year of *Back to the Future* itself—1985. And back then, only 340,000 people in the US had cell phones.

Forget today's world for a moment. Forget today's computers which can perform thousands of complex tasks—and even respond to your verbal query. Forget about Amazon. Forget the idea of anyone anywhere being willing or able to key in a credit card for an online purchase. And definitely forget artificial intelligence.

Technically speaking, the history of domain names starts before 1985 because the first domain names were Usenet names used by universities for internal communications. So while they existed, it's not how we would think of a domain name today.

In terms of how we would generally view domain names today, Verisign, the registrar who owns .COM, launched on January 1, 1985. Two months later, on March 15, 1985, Symbolics.com became the first .COM to be registered. (Originally registered by Symbolics, Inc. which was a computer services company based in Cambridge, Massachusetts.)

Symbolics.com wasn't the first domain name ever registered, though. That honor belongs to Nordu.net, which was registered on January 1, 1985.

Strange as it may sound, you didn't have to pay to register a domain name back then! After all, the internet wasn't yet in the mainstream. Instead, you sent in a letter via snail mail to Verisign to request the domain name you wanted. If it was available, you would then receive a letter back confirming you were the registrant. The first such letter of confirmation we know about was for Air.com.

By the time the '90s rolled around, people began registering domain names by the bucketloads, realizing they might one day have value. Turns out they were right. One famous story involved a businessman named Yun Yi from Vancouver, Canada who bought a collection of domain names, sold them later to Marchex to the tune of $34 million and then disappeared off the grid.

One of the early pioneers I've had the pleasure of meeting is Kevin Ham. In the '90s, he had finished med school but then decided to put off residency so he could invest in domain names instead. In an article about him titled "The Man Who Owns the Internet," he talked about the early days of collecting domain names. It was back in the dialup era, and he would have five computers going at once—he'd start the registration for one name on the first computer and while it was processing, move to the next, and so on—a sort of "assembly line" for domain registration.

He quickly developed better systems by generating a script and then automating the process so he could add more and more to his collection. Over time, he amassed a portfolio of over 200,000 domain names, many of them premium-level names.[12] In 2017, he sold these to GoDaddy for a reported $50 million.[13] (Side note: Kevin has published some content at Ham.com, which I'd encourage you to read.)

Speaking of GoDaddy, they have become the "big kahuna" in the industry by amassing a portfolio of domain names valued in the *billions*. And they continue to accrue value as assets.

This is also when we saw the beginning of *cybersquatting*. In other words, people would buy up domain names for known entities, hoping they could then force those entities to buy the domain name for large sums. One of the most famous—or rather, infamous—is the case of "White House" .COM. The registrants knew many people searching for information would type in .COM instead of .GOV—the actual site for the White House—and unfortunately, this exposed many people, especially children, to explicit adult content.

Other somewhat-less nefarious examples included people buying up available names for famous individuals and then selling ad space on those sites, knowing people would end up there looking for info on their famous musician, author, or artist. These questionable practices eventually led to the creation of ICANN in 1998 to work with the US government to establish policies and protocols around internet safety and ethical rules for domain name registration.

The names that interest me the most as a broker are those registered before 2000 because that was the heyday of "the new gold rush." Many of these domain names didn't resolve at all or if they did they were simply "parked pages," meaning there was no associated website or service to access, but the domain name displayed some ads that, when clicked, made the registrant a little money. Most were simply being held for future use by the registrant. By the late '90s, we saw the birth of Google and people began buying domain names to use for e-commerce purposes. In doing so, domain names moved from being just a niche aspect of online trade to becoming intricately woven with a company's brand.

In 2000, of course, we saw the Dotcom Bust where some pundits declared "the internet was over." As we know now, the bust was just the result of growing pains in the digital revolution. Many people let their domain names expire at that time—while others doubled down and bought up as many as they could manage.

As the internet grew, so did the number of TLDs (See Chapter 1) and I expect we'll continue to see new TLDs come and go. But to this day, .COM remains the gold standard and that's never going to change.

In the next chapter, we'll dive into all the various players who have emerged from the history of domain names—from the registrars, to the brokers like myself, to investors and buyers, and more. When you know the players, then you're better equipped to play the game.

CHAPTER 3

THE PLAYERS IN THE DOMAIN NAME INDUSTRY

THE FIRST ROLE I ever played in my own history with domain names was that of a buyer—it's just too bad I bought a crappy domain name. While I didn't know back then how deeply entrenched I would become with this business, it gave me the opportunity to interact with one of the other major players—the registrar—and learn how the registration process works.

Since then I've also become an investor, a seller, and a broker. My work as a broker has taken me across the world to conferences and auctions where I've had the chance to rub elbows with many others in the industry, including the journalists who help get the word out about the major happenings within the industry.

To keep things simple, though, I want to hone in on the key players:

- Registrars
- Domain Brokers
- Buyers/Investors
- Journalists
- Service Providers

REGISTRARS

The word registrar may bring up memories for some of you of being in college and registering for your classes—and finding out how much you'll have to pay each semester. It's an apt analogy for us because in the domain name industry, it's the registrars you use to "own" the domain names in the same way a university could be said to "own" the classes. You register for classes and in exchange you get the credit for completing them. Drop the class and you don't get the credit.

Likewise, as mentioned back in Chapter 1, you never actually *own* a domain name—you are credited as the registrant. But if you let that registration lapse, it reverts to the registrar—or to whoever snaps up the registration when it becomes available. When you have a domain name registered to you, you're building on "leased land," assuming you have an operating website to go with the domain name.

While there are a number of registrars, the leader in the field is GoDaddy. Founded in 1998, they have claimed the top spot in the industry not only because of their *eighty-four million* registered domain names[14] (representing a 14 percent market share[15]) but also through strategic acquisitions of high-value domain names and associated services like web hosting.

Established in 2001, Namecheap is another popular registrar with ten million registered domain names, in addition to email and web hosting services. Interestingly enough, both GoDaddy and Namecheap are based in Phoenix, Arizona, *not* Silicon Valley as one might expect.

Some registrars are more regionally-focused, such as Fabulous,[16] an Australia-based registrar which focuses on the .AU TLD (acquired by GoDaddy in 2017). Back when Fabulous started, GoDaddy wasn't yet focused on an international market, which allowed for companies like Fabulous to establish themselves alongside emerging ccTLDs.

Other registrars of note which you may have heard of include:

- Network Solutions
- IONOS
- Bluehost
- DreamHost
- Hover
- Hostinger
- Dynadot
- NameSilo

It's important we distinguish registrars from *registries*. Registries refer to companies who own a TLD. For instance, Verisign is the owner of the .COM registry, so if GoDaddy is interested in a list of .COM domain names, they must do so through Verisign.

However, a registrar could buy an entire registry as an investment asset. For instance, in 2020, GoDaddy bought the following registries: .US, .BIZ, .IN, and .CO. And in 2021, they bought .CLUB and the MMX portfolio of twenty-eight domain extensions. These acquisitions make GoDaddy a vertically-integrated company because they operate as a registrar while also owning these registries. They make money by both *owning* the name and by *executing* the registration for the name.

Anyone can go to GoDaddy or Namecheap or any other registrar and register an available domain name, so it begs the logical question—why in the world would you need a broker?

BROKERS

Imagine for a moment you're sitting on your couch, enjoying your favorite show or cheering for your favorite team, and you hear a knock at the door. Let's say you get up and open the door.

Standing on your front porch is a person you've never seen before. At first, you think maybe it's a new neighbor who's come by to introduce themselves—or maybe someone looking for their lost pet. But then they say, "I've driven by your house a few times and love this property! It's on the lake, it's got a great view, the schools nearby are fantastic, and it's close to where I work. I'd like to buy it from you."

While I can't predict how you'd react to this, I know how I would. After thanking them for their interest, I'd say, "Thanks but our home isn't for sale."

But let's say one day I'm working and get an email from a real estate agent I know: "David, This may seem out of the blue, but I was wondering if you'd ever considered selling your house? I have a current client looking for a property just like yours and is willing to pay 25 percent over market value. Would you be open to chatting?"

In real estate, when someone offers more—and sometimes far more—than the appraised value, it's called a "Make Me Move" offer.

Well, now things just got interesting. It doesn't mean I would sell—moving is such a hassle, after all. And I'm also at that stage in my life where I like to say I'm living in my "forever" or "last stop" home, and we're emotionally and financially invested in the house. But I'm far more likely to entertain this kind of offer from a trusted broker than a random stranger showing up at my door.

Brokers provide a similar service when it comes to domain name acquisitions. Domain names are "digital real estate," after all—and some deals require a level of industry savviness to handle. A brand new real estate agent probably can't sell a $10 million home yet—they need to gain more experience first. But more importantly, it takes decades to learn how to negotiate with sellers and buyers at this level. The same could be said of agents who specialize in commercial properties or multifamily units. These deals have nuances to them and it's no different for domain names.

For instance, let's say a US-based corporation is launching a new service. The corporation may want the new service to have its own brand identity separate from the parent company. So they go online, conduct a search, and find out the domain name they want is already owned by someone else. Then they'll reach out, find out the seller's asking price, come to an agreement, and then commence with buying the domain name and completing the transaction.

But then two months later, they find themselves in court against the US federal government—because it turns out the seller they negotiated with is based in Iran. And the embargo against Iran means they just violated federal law. Not a good situation to land in.

Or let's say you are negotiating with someone for a domain name, reach a price, and you send the money over. Days go by and you discover you still don't have the domain name. You reach out—and hear nothing. The emails are getting no reply and the seller has disappeared from the face of the earth. Turns out you just got scammed—and to make matters worse, the "seller" you negotiated with was never the owner of the domain name in the first place. So you have no legal right to the domain name even though you sent someone money.

Brokers can save you from both mistakes—and many more. Because of the valuation of the asset class, you need a broker who understands the market, understands the pitfalls, and can help you navigate complex negotiations and transactions.

In my work, I've done plenty of international deals. In the span of a day, I can be on the phone with a buyer in Australia, a seller in China, and an investor in the US. Bidding wars over premium domains can see offers coming in rapid-fire from around the globe—and if you don't have someone in your corner, you could miss out on the name you're looking for or a big sale you're hoping to make.

This is especially true when the domain name you want isn't "for sale." If the name is important to your brand and growth (and it should be, see Section II), then you need someone who can help you track down who the name is registered to and see if they are open to selling. They're far more likely to entertain a proposal coming through an established broker than an unsolicited request.

In the event you're pursuing an international transaction, knowing the cultural nuances of negotiation can make or break the deal. Several years ago, I was hired by a client to pursue an acquisition where the seller was in China. I had done over a hundred deals in China, so I had already learned some important aspects of respecting their culture regarding negotiation: Be direct, be firm, and show no signs of indecisiveness or weakness.

Since I don't speak Mandarin or Cantonese and can't write in Simplified or Traditional Chinese, I hired someone to translate my emails for me into Simplified Chinese. My usual translator was already booked up, so I tried someone new. Within a very short period of time, replies started coming back to me with a different tone than the one I'm used to seeing with Chinese contacts.

Everything felt wrong. The domain owner was acting like this was my first negotiation and they were replying with aggressive and domineering tones I rarely see in negotiations these days. Something was off. What had I done wrong?

To find out, I was able to get my first choice translator to have a look at the negotiation. I discovered that this new translator had not actually been interpreting my responses correctly. He had been adding in niceties like "sorry," "please," and "thank you," along with other extra words I never actually said. While these manners work great in my home state of Georgia, they are all seen as a sign of weakness in a negotiation with someone from China.

When I asked the new guy why he had done this, he responded that my initial tone was too harsh, so he softened it up during translation. *Ugggh!* Not what you ever want someone to do for you in a high-stakes negotiation where *every* word carries weight.

So with the help of my original translator, I cleared the air. I had her explain exactly what had happened and provided my original text so the domain owner knew *exactly* what I had originally said with the intended tone. We carried on the negotiation, with my original translator capturing the essence of my words correctly, and the deal moved forward.

A key lesson stands out from this incident and hundreds of other discussions with Chinese buyers and sellers. One tactic used by some Chinese negotiators is called *má fan*. If you think you have a deal and, at the last minute, a change is thrown in, that's *má fan*. It literally translates to "complications," and some negotiators like to throw new items into a discussion just to see if they can get more money from a buyer or a further reduced price from a seller.

So now, if I ever feel like I'm getting run over by a bus during a negotiation and the other party is in China, I'll sometimes reply simply with "No *má fan*." The level of instant respect you get as a Westerner is noticeable if that's indeed what's been happening, and I've used this phrase a few times to salvage multi-million dollar negotiations.

Psychology weighs heavily in negotiations—especially if you're wanting to acquire a legacy name from someone. Even if they are not actively using the domain anymore, they may have an emotional attachment to it—it might be the person's first or last name, or perhaps it was their old family email server, or the name of the business they ran before they retired. Often, the hesitance to sell is not about the money—it's about the *emotional attachment* they have to the name itself.

Returning to the example of houses, it's like offering market value for someone's house when they **don't** have a "For Sale" sign out. The house is more than property to them—it's personal. It represents their memories, their family, their life.

For instance, I once reached out to a domain owner to see if he was interested in selling. In response, he wrote, "David, I've had this domain name for over thirty years. When I bought it, I was single and now I've got grandkids. It's the only email address I've ever used." For him, the name meant so much more than just a collection of letters on a screen— it represented his entire adult life!

Likewise, if the domain name belongs to a business, it may represent the brand or one of their products. Even if they don't have a developed website at the domain name, they may have associated trademarks—or a ton of merch made up with that name. So you can't view it as trying to buy an "unused" domain name from them.

In either case, opening the door to a sale means getting into their head to understand their level of attachment to the domain name. As a broker, I often have to help people mentally let go of the name before any kind of negotiation can proceed. Otherwise, no amount of money will change their mind.

There are multiple levels to such a negotiation which experienced brokers can navigate. Often, I help guide such sellers to emotionally detach by trying to figure out what they could do with the money from the purchase. Maybe they want a new car, or pay off the mortgage, or travel more, or pay for college for their grandchildren, or create a foundation for a cause they believe in.

As a broker, I help them see how selling the domain name could actually fund these dreams. By understanding what's important to them, I can guide them in creating a new emotional connection to the *outcome*, not just a dollar sign. If the domain name is owned by a business, it's no different: I also try to help them visualize what a sizable influx of cash could do for their business.

As an acquisition broker, I have a responsibility to our client to acquire the domain name for them at a price they're willing to pay. But with domain owners, it isn't always about the price.

For instance, many sellers want to make sure they aren't selling their name to something they don't agree with morally. They don't want their old domain being used for an adult website or gambling or a hate group.

It can work in the other direction, too—a buyer who is reluctant to purchase a domain name which could benefit their brand but may have been previously associated with a vice. For example, I was once speaking on the phone to a new prospect, a super sweet grandmother who I liked immediately. She wanted to sell her two-letter, high-value .COM domain.

As we spoke, I typed the domain name into my browser—and then said, "Whoa!"

In response to my visceral reaction, she replied, "I'm sorry dear, I should've mentioned that I was in the adult entertainment industry . . . "

We got the engagement, marketed the asset globally, and ended up in negotiations with an interested buyer overseas. But since adult entertainment sites were banned in the prospective buyer's country, they were reluctant to move forward. As a broker, I was able to help negotiate the terms to make sure all the content would be removed and that we could divorce the domain name from the banned vice. In the end, we were able to work out an agreeable deal where everyone was happy.

These are just some of the sensitive and complex types of deals which we brokers see day-in, day-out.

I also help founders and entrepreneurs obtain financing for high-value domain name investments. That's right—just like buying a home or a business purchase, you can finance a domain name. This actually happens a lot more than you might suspect, even for domain names with seven-figure valuations.

We'll talk about this more later in Chapter 5, but it's worth quickly noting how amazing these finance deals can be for both parties. In my experience, the entrepreneurs of scrappy startups who finance their domain names are the least likely to default on their payments. They value the domain name so much, they'll sell their house and crash on a friend's couch before they will let go of the name! They also tend to be the most successful—they're driven to success because they want to keep the domain name at all costs.

Since there are no industry-wide rules, brokers largely set their own fees for the transactions they handle for clients, sort of like in real estate. Even so, 15 percent of the final sales price is considered fairly standard. GoDaddy also has some brokerage services and charges up to 25 percent unless you are using other services as well, and then they drop the percentage.

Certainly you can find some "discount brokers" out there who only charge around 10 percent, but these are often newer brokers still lacking in experience or they only handle certain, easier transactions. Often, their business model is based on high volume and automation. Like most of life, you get what you pay for. The level of service you'll receive from lower-end brokers isn't anywhere near the same level of finesse or knowledge you'll get from an experienced broker, especially when you reach the negotiation stage.

More importantly, you need a broker with the business acumen and experience to speak to the C-Suite—someone who can get the potential seller *to* the table in the first place. When you're looking at a sale or purchase that's $50K and upwards, you're not going to get the best deal with a discount broker.

When meeting with a prospective client, whether they are buying or selling, I have one consistent message: "No one will work harder for you to get the best deal for you." I can say this confidently because there's no feeling in the world like helping two parties find a deal that works for everyone. It's why I love what I do.

BUYERS & INVESTORS

My journey to becoming a broker began by first being a buyer and then an investor in domain names. As mentioned in the Introduction, my first experience as a domain name buyer was buying the domain for MarTech, but my mindset back then was only functional, not strategic. We had no idea what we were doing, no brand strategy. We just needed an address for the website as a "necessary evil" and then the digital revolution taught us a difficult lesson.

When I learned about domain names as an investment strategy, my thinking became far more strategic. I filled up a spreadsheet with 18,252 high-value name ideas and started reaching out to the owners of these already-registered names to see what price point they might be willing to sell for.

There's money to be made if you find eager sellers and buyers in an illiquid market.

Remember back in grade school how you learned that all squares are rectangles—but not all rectangles are squares? It's the same idea here with buyers and investors.

Anyone who has the registration for a domain name is technically a buyer because they had to pay for the registration. But not every buyer is an investor.

Real estate can help us here, too. Both homeowners and real estate investors have to purchase the property they want. But the intention of the homeowner is to live there. Meanwhile, the investor may want to lease out the property—or flip it. It's the same in the domain industry.

When I got serious about domain names, I was buying most domains as a long-term strategy. But I was also "flipping" some names for liquidity. I'd take the earnings from one sale and use it to pick up some other names I was really interested in long-term. Then, as you might recall, when I decided to branch out on my own and start up Brannans.com, I had to go out and negotiate for the name because it wasn't available so I could use it as my own business home page.

Remember, as a buyer, you can think of your domain name as your "digital front door." But as an investor, you think of them as assets which accumulate value over time, like a stock portfolio.

Investors want to bring liquidity to the transaction. If they spent $200,000 to get the name, they don't want to let it go for less than $500,000. Sometimes they get really lucky and a brand comes along who *really* wants the name they own and is willing to cough up big money for it.

Many investors become savvy about knowing when someone needs liquidity and is therefore more willing to part with a premium name at a lower cost. They're buying low so they can sell high.

For instance, I once worked with a bank who ended up turning down an exact match one-word .COM—which could have been theirs for only six figures. It was a steal! But they ignored my advice and believed the common myths, "We don't need the .COM" and "We'll wait to see if we can snatch it up for a lower price."

Spoiler alert . . .

Their plan backfired.

An investor came in and got the name instead, with the plan to hold onto it until they could at least 10X its sale. Do you think that bank will ever be able to get that name for six-figures again? Not in a million years. And their brand only suffered as a result. Owning the exact match .COM isn't just a marketing signal to all who go to the website, it increases the brand's footprint, the quality of traffic, and the conversion rate for sales.

I've seen this scenario play out more times than I can count—where a large corporation misses out on the prime brand-match domain name, and instead, an investor or speculator gets it instead.

For my part, I feel like I do a disservice to my clients by selling to investors. Why? Because when an investor is interested in it, then I know there's a good chance the name can accrue further value for my client by selling to someone else, like a corporate entity or a startup who can use the name. But sometimes, when you're needing liquidity, then selling to an investor can be a way to put cash in your pocket quickly.

Corporate buyers will generally be the highest bidder. These are the entities and startups who want an exact match domain (EMD) for their brand. They are looking long-term at how the domain name will help them establish their corporate identity, advance their brand, and drive traffic to their website as part of their sales strategy.

Ring.com is such an example. It's a far more desirable brand name than their original—DoorBot.com. But as you can imagine, they weren't the only company who would want a name like "Ring." The name could've also been put to good use by someone in the jewelry business, telecommunications, or even in the wedding industry. When similar names go on the market, they tend to set off a bidding war, driving the price higher than many investors are willing to go.

If you're a domain name buyer who wants to "live" in your domain name, who wants to use it to grow your brand and establish your identity in the marketplace—all the more reason for you to enlist a broker. Trying to chase it yourself could mean you never get to the negotiation table, miss out on a bid, or lose out to an investor who's only going to hike up the price. Plus, a broker can help you work out the details of any kind of finance plan, email forwarding, or other seller-based restrictions with the current holder.

JOURNALISTS

Journalists in the domain industry are a rare breed—and essential for helping move the market forward. One of the leading journalists is Ron Jackson, the editor and publisher of Domain Name Journal (DNJournal. com) who started reporting on the industry way back in 2003. According to his ICANN bio, he started buying up domain names for himself in 1997 and then "recognized the need for a specialized publication for the quickly growing industry."[17]

Like journalists in any other industry, they report on major transactions and any regulatory happenings which could disrupt the market. I personally hold a lot of respect for Ron as an excellent interviewer and because he never relies on clickbait like you see in other sectors.

The reporting in the industry plays a massive role in valuation and how prices increase over time. I'd encourage you to take a look at a chart on our website (Brannans.com) showing how valuation has gone up over the last few decades:

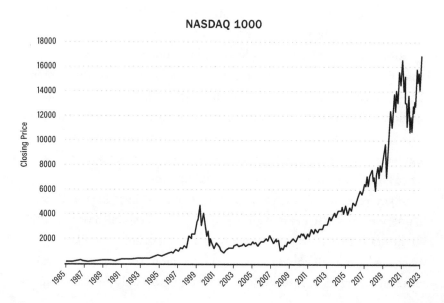

NASDAQ 1000

Domain Name	Selling Price	Domain Name	Selling Price
Cars.com*	$872,000,000	FB.com	$8,500,000
LasVegas.com	$90,000,000	RealEstate.com	$8,500,000
CarInsurance.com	$49,700,000	HealthInsurance.com	$8,130,000
Vegas.com	$38,000,000	WE.com	$8,000,000
Insurance.com	$35,600,000	Business.com	$7,500,000
VacationRentals.com	$35,000,000	Diamond.com	$7,500,000
PrivateJet.com	$30,200,000	Beer.com	$7,000,000
Voice.com	$30,000,000	Z.com	$6,800,000
Batteries.com	$20,500,000	iCloud.com	$6,000,000
Bookings.com	$20,000,000	Israel.com	$5,900,000
Internet.com	$18,000,000	Casino.com	$5,500,000
360.com	$17,000,000	Slots.com	$5,500,000
Insure.com	$16,000,000	Toys.com	$5,100,000
Chat.com	$15,500,000	AsSeenOnTv.com	$5,100,000
NFTs.com	$15,000,000	Snap.com	$5,000,000
Fab.com	$15,000,000	SEO.com	$5,000,000
Bankaholic.com	$15,000,000	Property.com	$5,000,000
Rocket.com	$14,000,000	Korea.com	$5,000,000
Sex.com	$14,000,000	Clothes.com	$4,900,000
Fund.com	$12,000,000	Medicare.com	$4,800,000
IRS.com	$12,500,000	IG.com	$4,700,000
Tesla.com	$11,000,000	AV.com	$4,200,000
Hotels.com	$11,000,000	Marijuana.com	$4,200,000
CardRatings.com	$10,200,000	GiftCard.com	$4,000,000
Connect.com	$10,000,000	Freeporn	$4,000,000
Fund.com	$10,000,000	YP.com	$3,900,000
Porn.com	$9,500,000	IT.com	$3,800,000
Shoes.com	$9,000,000	HG.com	$3,800,000
Porno.com	$8,900,000	MI.com	$3,600,000
Gold.com	$8,515,000	Ice.com	$3,500,000

*Cars.com - Did not trade hands for this amount. The company placed this value on the domain name in SEC filings. They listed it as an indefinite-lived intangible asset.

In Chapter 1, I mentioned data about how we can be certain .COM is the gold standard TLD. Well, here it is. A quick run through the list and you'll see that almost every single domain name listed is a .COM.

As of writing, five million sales totaling $2.7 billion have been reported in the industry.[18] And while not all transactions are publicly available for journalists to report on, their work helps brokers, sellers, and buyers alike gauge potential in the names they are pursuing. For instance, at the time of writing, the largest valuation for a domain name is $872 million for Cars.com based on SEC filings in 2015. (To be clear, this is not what the domain name sold for as some online sources will say.)

The second highest valuation on the list is LasVegas.com which we're going to discuss more in Section 2—valued at $90 million way back in 2005. Vegas.com went for a cool $38 million in 2015.

Some of my favorite journalists in the industry include:

- Ron Jackson, who runs DNJournal.com
- Andrew Allemann, who runs DomainNameWire.com
- Elliot Silver, who runs DomainInvesting.com
- Raymond Hackney, who runs TheDomains.com
- Michael Gilmour, who runs WhizzBangsBlog.com
- George Kirikos, who is not technically a journalist but contributes immensely to the industry by reading SEC disclosure reports and reporting on domain name transactions.
- And a special mention to Theo Develegas, who runs DomainGamg.com, which also has some great satire along with solid reporting.

Some other well-known sites you should know about:

- DomainIncite.com
- JamesNames.com
- And international-based sites like AcornDomains.co.uk (UK-centric reporting), Domain-Recht.ed (German reporting), Dodong.com (Korean reporting), NameTribune.com (Spanish), and News.srl (Italian).

Without journalists, the industry would remain more "in the dark" than what it already is. If you're considering domain names as an investment asset or as a buyer for your brand, you'd do well to pay attention to the reporting here and keep your finger on the pulse of the industry.

SERVICE PROVIDERS

Finally, as in any industry, you'll also find a number of service providers who interact with domain names and assist with various aspects. Think of any time you've gone to an industry conference or trade show and how many booths and sponsors you'll see everywhere. Likewise, the domain industry has its own conferences and trade shows, such as NamesCon, a conference geared specifically for buyers, sellers, and investors.

In general, there are eight types of individuals/companies you will see at such conferences:

- Registries (ex: Verisign)
- Registrars (ex: GoDaddy)
- Investors (individuals and companies)
- Brokers (ex: Brannan's)
- IP Lawyers (ex: John Berryhill)
- Brand Protection Agencies (ex: CSC or MarkMonitor, which we will discuss further in Chapter 4)
- Governing Bodies (ex: ICANN)
- Brands & Startups

Since we've already covered Registries, Registrars, Investors, and Brokers thoroughly, let's turn our attention to the other groups here, starting with IP Lawyers and Brand Protection Agencies.

IP LAWYERS

Lawyers who specialize in intellectual property are a massive piece of the puzzle in the industry—and they don't often get the due they deserve. Hardly a week goes by when I'm not speaking with an IP lawyer about some issue or other.

At time of writing, there are a number of IP attorneys I have recommended to clients, including:

- John Berryhill
- David Weslow
- Paul Keating
- Ari Goldberg
- Karen Bernstein
- Stevan Lieberman
- Zak Muscovitch
- Jason Schaeffer

So why should you specifically seek out an IP lawyer with experience in domain names?

Short answer: Because domain names are an entirely different animal than your typical IP.

Domain names fall under the category of intellectual property known as an indefinite lived, intangible asset. In some cases, it ends up being the most valuable asset a company owns, which is why it occasionally requires some legal protection like any other piece of property.

We'll touch on these ideas more in Chapter 6. For now, it's enough to know that companies and individuals who are looking to upgrade their domain name, sell an unused "parked" domain name, or who are researching premium domain names to align with their brand should be aware of the IP and trademark issues to be considered. Since I am not a legal expert in those matters, you should always reach out to an IP lawyer to get advice!

BRAND PROTECTION AGENCIES

As you might imagine, as long as domain names have existed, there have been bad actors who want to try to weaponize or steal them. This can include someone purchasing an available domain name for a well-known celebrity or brand in the hopes they can essentially hold it "ransom" and get a big payday in exchange.

While an IP lawyer is going to be useful should you ever need to pursue legal action, brand protection agencies come in extremely useful for ongoing brand protection needs.

Corporation Service Company (CSC) is unique in our industry because they are over 125 years old, but they have provided legal services to some of the largest brands in the world, from Apple in the tech space to Toyota in automotive to Walt Disney in entertainment. In the digital landscape, they've developed a reputation for helping companies protect themselves from such bad actors and be able to safeguard their trademarks—old and new—through domain name protection and acquisition.

CSC is not the only company that brands turn to for protecting their IP, though. MarkMonitor, Safebrands, Brandsight (purchased by GoDaddy), and Marksmen are all reputable brand protection agencies, well-established in the domain name industry.

So let's say Ford Motor Company decided to resurrect their Panther line as a hybrid called the Ford Panther Eco. Some bad actors out there might think they can profit by registering a domain name like FordPantherEco.com. Not only would this be a terrible domain name choice, but the person who does so would land themselves in hot water as Ford Motor Co. would move to protect their brand.

Brand protection agencies come in to help brands protect their IP, including any trademark infringement tips. And not just major corporations—I once knew a dentist who enlisted help because a bad actor was trying to take his name. Some bad actors do this to scam people out of their money—they'll register a domain name similar to the brand people know—and then request information or payment of some kind.

Getting an email from a brand protection agency (see Chapter 3 and 10) can mean a couple of things: Either they are looking into you infringing on a client's property, or perhaps they have a client wanting to buy your domain name for some plans they have. It's not unusual for these agencies to send out notices on behalf of their clients, making five-figure offers. If you ever get such an offer from any of these agencies, do some research and reach out to a broker. Find out if your domain might have even *more* value than what they're offering.

GOVERNING BODIES

In the domain industry, the primary governing body to know is ICANN since they set out many of the international regulations which should be followed. They are also responsible for deciding which new TLD registries can be created.

But buyers and sellers alike should also be aware of other international laws, such as the embargo scenario mentioned before. If you're doing a domain name transaction between international parties, then you need to make sure you're also abiding by any laws for both nations related to cybersecurity and trade. Basically, if you send money internationally, you need to make sure you're compliant with sanctions set by the Office of Foreign Assets Control (OFAC). US banks will follow KYC (Know Your Customer) and AML (Anti-Money Laundering) regulations so you need to make sure you're complying with those as well.

In addition to protecting your IP, an IP lawyer or brand protection agency can offer guidance in any legal quagmires you'll have to navigate. The last thing you want at the conclusion of a deal is to have agents from the FBI or ATF knocking on your door.

BRANDS & STARTUPS

Within the industry, you'll find a number of brands who provide various services, including:

- Web hosting providers (ex: Wordpress, Squarespace, Wix, etc.)
- Website design and maintenance services (On Budget Services)
- E-commerce transaction services (ex: Shopify, Stripe, Square, etc.)
- Cybersecurity services
- Parking services (ex: Parking Crew)

Parking services provide a small income stream for investors and companies who buy up domain names but are not actively using them.

Go to any domain name convention or conference and you'll find a slew of startup founders and entrepreneurs. Often, they are investigating and researching ideas for their brand. They might have the idea and business plan drawn up, but remember—words have power. They need to find that right word—or combination of words—which will grab interest and align with their mission.

They might attend an auction—if there is one—to see what names are already available – or they might even talk with sponsors and service providers to better understand the ins and outs of the domain industry. Much of the information I've included in this book comes from questions I've received from startup founders who are curious or from attendees and speakers of the 100-plus conferences I've hosted, been a partner of, or attended over the years.

Sometimes you'll even find individuals who want to get into the domain name business, so they are learning what other services are needed. They're talking to everyone, looking for a gap or bottleneck in the industry, with the sole intention of building a business to satisfy that specific pain point.

In a sense, they're living up to the famous quote by Sir Isaac Newton: "If I have seen further, it is by standing on the shoulders of giants." They want to stand on the shoulder of the current industry "giants" to better see the horizon of the business.

CONCLUSION

Where do you fit into the domain name industry? Do you see yourself as a buyer or investor? Or maybe a future broker? Or could you see yourself getting into IP law or starting a new service?

In the next chapter, we'll explore the different types of Domain Name Owners and their approaches. So whether you are trying to buy or sell a domain name doesn't matter here—you need to be able to understand how a domain owner *thinks*.

CHAPTER 4

DOMAIN NAME OWNERS

YOU MIGHT RECALL from Chapter 1 that we discussed how you never truly "own" a domain name unless you own the registry itself. However, for the sake of practicality, we still largely refer to registrants as "owners." It's a helpful distinction since when it comes to a transaction between two parties, the registrar is not making the sale directly—it's the owner of the registration and whoever is looking to buy it.

It's helpful to break up the categories of owners in terms of how each group thinks about their domain name. Their thinking will then determine their approach for how they use—or *not* use—the domain and whether they will ever be willing to part with it as an asset. In general, we see three types of owners:

- Individuals
- Corporations
- Investors

INDIVIDUALS

While my first experience of owning a domain name was with MarTech, I don't always like to count it. For one, because it was a disaster. But also because I was not the sole owner—the company owned the domain name and it only served a functional purpose for our fledgling business. The first time I truly became a domain name owner happened later on when I was attending Kennesaw State University.

The first domain name I bought where I was thoughtful and intentional about the purchase was DavidClements.com. I was taking an Intro to CSIS course (Computer Science and Information Systems) where I was required to develop a website using html coding. Instead of using one of the free domain names offered by the course, I decided to see if my own name was available as a domain. Who knew? Maybe I'd have a proper use for it later on.

Thankfully, my exact match SLD name "DavidClements" was still available for .COM. A guy in medical school named Ned was pretty tech savvy and had set up a registrar as a TuCows reseller, so he helped me host the name, which I've had since June 25, 2002. Starting then, Ned got money from me each year until I eventually moved the registration to a new registrar.

My thinking for the domain name was very functional—I didn't view the domain name as an investment. I needed it for the class and thought maybe one day I'd use it for my own personal email and maybe a website.

Within this category of buyers, you'll see two distinctions in today's marketplace—Founders and Legacy Owners.

FOUNDERS

These are your startup founders and entrepreneurs who have a business idea and want to snap up a domain name for their brand so they can start building their business around it. When the door security company Ring was first started, it was known as Door Bot, so founder Jamie Siminoff acquired DoorBot.com. The original intention for the device was being able to see who was at the door—Is it a delivery driver who needs a signature? A girl scout selling cookies? Or a solicitor? However, in the process of developing the product and pitching it to investors, Siminoff discovered a new, more attractive angle—home security. This gave the device a new angle from being a "nice-to-have" product of convenience to a "must-have" product of necessity.

Now, this didn't mean the device couldn't still be used to see who was at the door—but security was the more marketable angle. This meant he needed a catchier, easy-to-spell, memorable name to build the brand around—Ring.

Jamie already knew about premium domain names and he under-stood how powerful Ring.com would be for his brand. Ring.com is the better name, not just because it is easy to remember, but because it could help attract both customers *and* investors. He also raised a little money to get Ring.com, but my point is that even *before* Doorbot, he had a collection of domain names because he knew they were valuable assets.

While your domain name should align with your overall business plan and strategy, it's also not a bad idea to grab domains while you can—especially if you can get .COMs. If you end up changing direction, you can always list them for sale (often for a profit) and move forward with the winning domain name for your brand.

LEGACY OWNERS

Simply put, these are the people who registered a domain name years ago and haven't let it go for twenty-plus years. Often these are family names which they have used for a family email server or a family business—or they just thought it would be fun to have a .COM behind their name.

The oldest ones I've seen go back to the early '90s when you could still acquire them for next to nothing because the internet wasn't mainstream yet. I've even seen situations where someone only discovered the domain name's existence while managing an estate after a loved one's passing. Sometimes this can end up becoming the most valuable asset in the entire estate.

Such legacy owners often aren't driven by money, though. As discussed in Chapter 3, there's typically an emotional attachment to the name. Getting these types of owners to detach from owning the names means first helping them to detach the corresponding emotion. You have to help them see how the funds from selling could be used for whatever else is important to them.

CORPORATE

You can't truly do business at scale without a website—and you can't have a website without a domain name. So the real question here is why corporations acquire domain names and who is behind the acquisitions?

Often, the conversation of acquiring a new domain is started by people in the marketing and branding departments. Let's say a new product or service is coming out soon—they might see the benefit in owning the associated domain name. My opinion is biased, of course, but it makes sense for brands to prioritize the domain over other kinds of brand promotion.

For instance, consider Poppi, the prebiotic soda. They spent around $7 million to have a Super Bowl commercial in 2024, but when you Google them, you'll quickly discover they don't own their exact match .COM. Instead, their website is DrinkPoppi.com.

Certainly, we don't know the behind-the-scenes story here. Perhaps they tried to acquire the .COM but the current owner, Aron Meystedt, wouldn't sell at a price they were willing to pay.

You can find other cases where a company just doesn't "get" it, where the leadership team just doesn't see the value in an exact match .COM for their brand.

The point: If a company is willing to spend $7 million for a Super Bowl ad, they should own their exact match domain name for their brand even if it's Super Bowl ad money, too.

When it's a business that wants to scale, obtaining the .COM for their SLD should be a priority. For the sake of the corporate identity and brand, they should find a way to put together an acquisition.

But these are the type of brand naming decisions which corporations face every day when they are looking to position their products for success: "Should we spend big money on a one-time investment on an asset that will never go away? Or do we spend it on a commercial?" I'll say it again, they need to do both.

The bigger the company is, the more they're willing to pay to acquire a premium domain name. They will always have the largest offer on the table. I've seen many $200K purchases happen this way, depending on whether the seller is more interested in liquidity.

Corporations looking to acquire a domain name may enlist the help of a domain brokerage service like Brannans to approach the current owner—who might be a small business or an individual. Sometimes the owner is high-net worth and, therefore, an unmotivated seller.

It's not uncommon a corporation picks up domain names as part of a merger or acquisition. While those names may not need to be in active use any longer, they still have to make decisions on what to do with those assets. These are conversations which may begin with their cybersecurity team but easily end up with the C-suite. They want to make sure those domains are secure, that there is no underlying data with the names—especially with defunct email servers—which could be used by a hacker or other cybercriminal. The intellectual property director for the company may even have a say in what happens because of the IP potential.

Years ago, I knew the former IP Director at Hewlett-Packard (HP). One day, we were talking about a list of domain names they had acquired that weren't being used. I asked how HP got the names, and he told me how HP would buy multiple companies every quarter—and would then acquire any domain names those companies had owned.

Often, these acquisitions happen in layers. For instance, DEC—Digital Equipment Corporation—had been bought by Compaq Computers, which meant Compaq acquired domain names like Digital.com and DEC.com. But then HP acquired Compaq—so now they owned those names. In these situations, it's often the M&A team who has to be responsible for the acquisition and disposition of domain name assets.

If a corporation is considering selling a domain they own, they have to weigh the pros and cons of doing so—Who would be buying it? How do they intend to use it? Could it create a problem for the corporation? Should they hold onto the name for potential use in the future?

It's also not uncommon for companies to need a new domain name as they grow—especially the startups who launch from incubators like Y Combinator or Techstars. This can pose a number of legal obstacles for both corporations and startups alike, often around trademark law. Startups may also have to contend with having less-than-desirable domain names early on since they're the scrawny, scrappy new kid on the block—and they may have to navigate IP and trademark laws. (See Chapter 6 for the story of how Dropbox acquired Dropbox.com.)

No matter what, the decision to buy or sell a domain name is far more complicated for a corporation than it is for an individual with a business idea. But the common denominator is being able to put a price on the name and what it's worth. Which brings us to our final group of buyers.

INVESTORS

Looking back, I missed out on a great investment opportunity in 2000 with the Dotcom Bust. There were one-word names which people let expire that could have sold for millions later on. It would be several more years before I'd have the lightbulb moment of looking around my room and seeing "dot com" behind every item.

You might recall I began my own domain journey more as an investor, flipping names. I once bought a single-word .COM for $3,400 that I was able to turn into $34,000. Another time, I bought a domain for $3,000 and sold it for $90,000. While these sales don't happen often, you can probably see why many people choose to go the investor route.

Just because a domain name is not available, doesn't mean it's not for sale. Many domain names are not available for registration or up for auction, but they can still be bought. And sometimes, they can be bought without spending crazy money on them. Good domain names can sometimes be purchased in the 5-figure range.

When you see headline-making transactions, it's usually because big fish companies—your Fortune 500 types—are buying from smaller fish—small businesses and individuals. So if the idea of investing is appealing to you, remember this—there's always a bigger fish.

This idea works both in your favor and against you. It works in your favor when you can flip a name you acquired at low dollar to a corporation who needs it for their brand. It works against you when you're bidding on a name at auction and the big fish comes in and snaps it up.

There are tens of thousands of investors out in the marketplace flipping domain names—just like how I started. An important distinction you should know about is understanding the drop process. That is, many of these individuals are setting up systems in which they can watch for domain names getting dropped so they can grab them when they expire.

Usually, an available domain name only becomes visible in the marketplace when it's expired. If it's one with any kind of potential value, it will be grabbed fast. Many investors make use of drop services which will alert them whenever a name is about to expire or go to auction.

You can think of these services a little like if your real estate agent knows you're looking for a new property. With their insider knowledge, they can keep an eye out for "pocket listings"—properties that aren't yet on MLS but they know are about to hit the market. Then they call you up and say, "Hey, there's a new property I think you'll like that's not on MLS yet, let me send you the details and pictures. The seller may be willing to entertain an early offer." This gives you the competitive edge in getting the property before anyone else.

Likewise, drop services monitor availability down to the second the name becomes available—and allow the investor to register it within milliseconds. Investors can end up buying a name for a $79 investment and then turn around and sell it for $2000. Do this with enough frequency and it can become a profitable revenue stream. Some investors do this full-time, while others keep it as their "side gig."

How common is it for corporations to buy from investors? Very common. In fact, investors want to sell to companies because they know it will be the best offer they can get. This can require a high level of patience, though – waiting for years, continuing to keep the registration renewed, until the right corporate buyer comes along. Otherwise, you feel like you've left money on the table.

You'll find speculators in the industry who are gifted at guessing domain name valuation, all based on years of experience in domain name investing. The most successful investors really understand domain names *and* illiquid markets. Since there's no standardized appraisal process in the industry like in real estate, it often comes down to how badly someone needs to acquire the name—or how badly someone wants to sell it. Someone needing liquidity will settle for less cash. Meanwhile, if the seller has a $10 million home, don't expect them to part with the domain name easily. But if you need more insight into valuation of domain names, we'll go deeper into the subject in Chapter 5.

CONCLUSION

Returning to 1849, you saw similar groups of buyers in the Gold Rush. You had individuals going out, buying up some land and mining it themselves. You had corporations setting up trade posts, refineries, land speculation services, and so on. And then you had the investors who bought up land and then leased it out or sold it for profit once gold had been found.

The question facing any buyer is how to understand the value of the domain name you're considering. How can you know you're looking at gold and not pyrite? What are the methods being used in the industry to gauge valuation? In the next chapter, we'll look at these questions more closely so we can understand domain name valuations.

CHAPTER 5

UNDERSTANDING DOMAIN NAME VALUATIONS

I N THE PREVIOUS chapter, I briefly touched on the idea of domain name valuation and the role investors play, in addition to speculators, and organizations like CSC which works with corporations to help them with legal, tax, and IP issues. But how do you put a price on an intangible asset? Who sets the standards?

As usual, real estate can help us understand how domain name valuation works. Certain zip codes carry with them higher property valuation—considerations like desirable location, low crime rates, good schools, solid infrastructure—all these factors play a role. And just like how a property with multiple bids will see a bidding war, the same can happen with domain names.

But where is the baseline? How can prospective buyers and sellers begin to understand the value of a name before pursuing a deal? Especially when you consider there is no standard appraisal process.

Often, valuations come down to a matter of perspective—that is, "Beauty is in the eye of the beholder." Since this can sound arbitrary at first, we must first understand domains as an investment class asset.

DOMAIN NAMES AS INVESTMENT CLASS ASSETS

As discussed in Chapter 5, investors look at domain names like any other asset which accrues value over time. Certainly, not all domain names will 10X their value over time, but many do. As a collective class of assets, domain name valuation has increased on pace with real estate and the stock market.

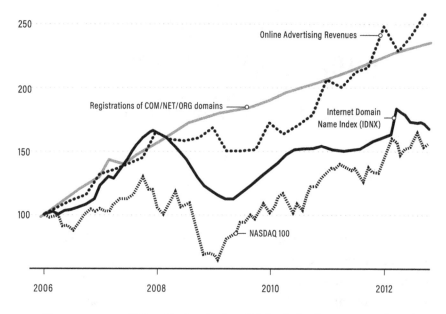

Ten years ago, Thies Lindenthal published the first comprehensive study looking into the valuation of domain names for MIT, entitled, "Valuable Words: The Price Dynamics of Internet Domain Names." As of the writing of this book, it remains a definitive reference point for many brokers like myself.

In the paper, Thies also compares domain names to "other investment classes such as stocks, bonds, or real estate," citing the risk factor and volatility. Note he doesn't say they are *more* volatile or risky—but simply they should be considered the same. I don't know of any financial advisors who would say *not* to invest in any stocks, bonds, or real estate. In any portfolio, diversification and longevity is the key—so why not throw domain names in, too?

Thies also points out how "any cautious economist will surely ask the following: Are domain names for real or just another fad? Or does an economic rationale justify the prices paid?"[19] If anything, the past ten years since the paper came out have answered these questions—domain names are here to stay and the economic rationale of the asset absolutely justifies the prices paid.

No one can guarantee a single domain name will skyrocket in value, of course, just as no one can guarantee a company stock will rise. But the overall trend is up and for those who retain their assets, the adage "good things come to those who wait" rings true.

Separate research from Escrow.com shows a similar story for the valuation of domain names. In fact, they go as far as to call domain names "the new 'virtual real estate.'"[20] In comparing the value of domain names to other digital assets like Bitcoin, they found "Unlike bitcoin, domain name prices have held a more moderate upward course in terms of growth without the volatility that has plagued the cryptocurrency."[21]

Despite this, we saw crypto take over headlines while domain name investing remained in the background. The same paper—published in 2018—showed domain name returns had experienced positive gains for seventeen years. The only major drop was the market crash of 2008-2009—which of course also affected the stock market and real estate market.[22]

Does this mean you should go out and buy up every single domain name you can get your hands on? Of course not. First, you need to understand what makes a name valuable. The Escrow report lays out many of the same price factors that I myself look at:

- Is it a .COM?
- How long is the domain?
- Is it easy to recall/remember?
- Does the domain have associated content?
- Does it align with a trending keyword or topic?

They use the cryptocurrency boom as an example of this last factor, citing how Crypto.com sold for an estimated $12 million in November of 2017 as bitcoin became the latest rage.[23] In terms of investment risk, domain names are pretty low, especially considering the limited cost to keep one year-to-year and the potential return for the right name.

DOMAIN NAME VALUATION

Context matters more than anything with valuing domain names—not only the name itself. Who the seller is, who the buyer is. Everything counts.

That said, it's at least helpful to be able to classify the type of valuations you might see. The following chart came from a speech by Paul Nicks—a figure in our industry who I trust for his knowledge and transparency. According to him, GoDaddy has a system they use where they rank domain names based on thirteen tiers of valuation. Given how many buckets of domain names and buyers are out there, breaking it into so many categories helps buyers and sellers alike know what they have on their hands.

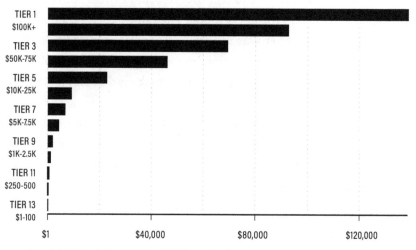

Source: GoDaddy Domain Name Value & Appraisal Tier System (2025)

For those of us who are experienced brokers, we're typically focused on helping clients whose deals fall in the top three tiers. Meanwhile, investors are going to be focused more on Tier 9 to Tier 7 for names they want to purchase and then flip. Startups or small businesses are often focused more on Tier 13 to Tier 10—going for lower value domain names.

You'll find exceptions, of course. Many future-thinking startups want to go for the Tier 1 name right off the bat because of the value to their brand and to drive interest and traffic. Some investors want to collect as many low-tier names as possible in hopes one of them becomes a top-tier unicorn that will pay off. It paid off for Ring.com, Scan.com, Slack.com, Stripe.com, Cart.com, etc.

BEWARE VALUATION TOOLS

A word of warning before we move on—don't trust online valuation tools. In general, I steer people away from all of these, which is why I won't even mention specific ones here. You can Google them easily enough if you want. But they're rarely helpful when it comes to an actual acquisition. You can never expect others to honor it, so citing a valuation tool in a negotiation is an excellent way to *not* be taken seriously.

The tools you'll find are automated guessers and should be taken with a heavy dose of salt. They can't take into account the nuances of domain names, especially when it comes to human behavior and psychology. A tool can tell you the name is worth $5K, but if the owner has had it for twenty years and spends their time jet setting between homes in three countries, don't bet on them caring one single bit what the valuation tool says.

Like I said earlier—beauty is in the eye of the beholder. This is the central tenet for domain name valuation. Much of the value comes down to the specific asset class it belongs to—intellectual property. How much is the IP and trademark worth to the owner? It might mean *everything* to them.

CHAPTER 6

INTELLECTUAL PROPERTY

SINCE DOMAIN NAMES fall under the asset class of intellectual property, it's important to have an understanding of IP and trademark law *before* pursuing a domain name acquisition. In fact, you should really be consulting an IP attorney with experience in trademark law to make sure you're on the up-and-up with an acquisition, because it's easy for things to go south if you don't know what you're doing.

Knowing and following IP law could make or break whether you get the premium domain name you're after. That's exactly what happened with Dropbox.

In their startup days, Dropbox's original domain was GetDropbox.com. Andrew Allemann wrote a fantastic article about this problem, based on an interview between author Tim Ferris and Dropbox co-founder Drew Houston, which I'll summarize for you.

Early on, Dropbox's leadership tried to play nice with the domain owner—bringing him champagne, talking up the VC funding they had just received, and explaining why they wanted to acquire the domain. The owner wasn't interested, though.

When Dropbox had their public launch, the domain owner began receiving emails—people who wanted in on the beta launch. See, these people *assumed* Dropbox was the owner of Dropbox.com. Which underscores why you need the exact name match when you can get it!

The owner became annoyed at the influx of emails, so he added Whois privacy to block his contact info. In a more hostile move, he then parked the domain with ads for Dropbox's competitors. Which was a mistake.

You can't just take away a domain name from a registrant for this, but they had the ability to sue the domain owner because of his decision to place competing ads on the site. The confusion it caused consumers had now become a legal issue they could act on—so they sued the domain name owner.

Eventually, the Dropbox team offered the owner two options—cash or stock. He chose settling for $300,000...though Houston claims if he'd taken the stock option, it would now be worth in the hundreds of millions.[24]

The obstacle facing many new domain name owners is they haven't done the leg work to examine the IP side of the domain name. They might accidentally infringe on someone else's trademark—or sometimes, intentionally do so and find themselves in a hefty lawsuit.

DOMAIN NAMES AS AN ASSET

It's first important to remember that domains not only serve a functional use but exist as an indefinite-lived, intangible asset. In accounting practice, "intangible" simply means it is not a physical asset—you can't hold it. "Indefinite-lived" refers to the concept that it does not lose value like other assets, nor is there a specific end date for the asset.

This is an asset class which applies specifically to intellectual property (IP), trademarks, and patents. According to the SEC, "The Company's trademarks and trade names are expected to generate cash flows indefinitely."[25] Or to put it another way, the name itself holds great value because of what it represents.

For instance, the most expensive domain name valuation at time of writing is Cars.com, which the corporation valued at $872 million in an SEC filing when it was acquired in 2014 by Gannett.[26] As an indefinite-lived, intangible asset, Gannett's accountants can list it as its own line item since it provides significant value to the company.

The beauty of this asset class is the low carrying cost. For instance, an office building doesn't count as an indefinite lived asset because it will wear over time and require renovation and additional costs to keep it sound. Meanwhile, the cost of keeping up registration on a domain name is *very* low, especially when considering the value it provides to a brand.

My advice to founders and entrepreneurs in particular is to move beyond seeing their domain name for its functional use, but to truly see it as a company asset. One which has long-term potential value both for the brand as a whole and in its own existence.

LEGAL CLAIMS

Since I'm not a legal expert myself, much of the following information is thanks to a conversation I had with David Weslow, a preeminent IP attorney for domain names. Since IP and trademark laws can vary nation to nation, you should always consult with an IP attorney with any concerns and David is one who has represented some significant global cases.

When it comes to potential buyers of a domain name, there are two categories:

1. A company looking solely to purchase a domain name.
2. A company looking to acquire the domain name by force where there is a legal basis to do so.

In the first category, David explained the individual or company is typically looking for a domain which "corresponds to the English or plain language meaning." For instance, when Coca-Cola decided to launch Coca-Cola Zero, even with trademarking the term, they wouldn't be able to *force* the owner of Zero.com to relinquish the domain name to them.

I've seen people make this mistake...they go out, get the trademark and then think they can force the owner to give it to them. Instead, what they do is rile the owner, which further jacks up the price. It's what I like to call "the FU tax."

What people need to do, however, is to conduct due diligence to make sure the term is available so they're not infringing on someone else's trademark. David mentioned to me how often this comes up in branding discussions with companies. Often, the branding firm or marketing team will propose a slew of names, but they haven't always done the work to make sure the name is clear to use. If it's too similar to a name within the same category, it can create confusion—and therefore, a legal problem.

For instance, if Ford decided to release their own truck with the name "Tundra," even though it's a common use word, they will run into legal problems with Toyota. But Coke could release their own drink "Coke Tundra" and not face the same problem because they are in a different product category.

When companies are looking to add new trademarks, they may end up submitting twenty or so to the US Patent and Trademark Office, and they might get fifteen of them approved for use. For instance, Overstock got a trademark for O.com even though they didn't own the domain name— they did so preemptively, hoping one day it *would* become available.

Which brings us to the second category—companies who have a legal basis to take a domain name. David explained this is typically when a brand has had their trademark for ten years, but perhaps they never acquired the corresponding domain. This is where cybersquatting comes into play.

So let's say a cybersquatter decides to go register LukeSkywalker.com. They might think they could force LucasFilm to pay them for the name, since they are the people behind the character of Luke Skywalker. Instead, the Walt Disney Company (as the owner of LucasFilm) would have a legal basis to force the cybersquatter to surrender the domain.

Generally speaking, if a company has registered a generic dictionary word domain name that's ten to twenty years old, there's no legal claim someone can make to force a transfer. Even if the company never used the domain name or never got a trademark for their domain name, if it's a generic term, you can't chase them down for it. (Ex: Snow.com, Bird. com, Green.com.)

If a name is legally clear to use, you can use the US Patent and Trademark Office's trademark search system to look up what trademarks others already have on specific names or two-word terms. While this is easy and free to use, it's still recommended you use an attorney to help you with this so there is no misunderstanding with the results.

PRIVACY

Whenever you are looking to acquire a domain name that is not available, the first step is to find out who owns the domain name. There are a number of WHOIS databases online to search for the owner of a domain name. Referring back to the Dropbox story, you might recall this is how the original owner of the domain began receiving unsolicited emails about Dropbox—people assumed Dropbox.com was owned by Dropbox and reached out.

As you can imagine, many people don't want their information publicly available like this, so they obtain privacy protection. This happened on a large scale in 2018 when the EU passed the GDPR—General Data Protection Regulation. Once it was enacted, this law meant that registrars cannot show registrant contact information freely. The registrar has to lock your info to keep you from getting spam or unsolicited contact—especially from speculators.

While the law technically only applies to EU citizens, our industry is *very* international. Many outside of the EU follow similar protocol because registrars don't want to lose their customer base. Churn rate is a problem for registrars—70 percent of domains are not renewed annually, with 41 percent expiring and the other 29 percent getting registered by new users.[27]

Given this, many registrars have decided to hide everyone's info because, I think, it keeps their churn rate lower.

When I spoke with David about this, he weighed in on how essential it is to identify records with higher confidence—meaning if you see the registrant information is locked, it should be a red flag. You need to do a lot of leg work to verify who you're dealing with is actually the domain name owner.

In David's words, "It's so important to have a great domain purchase and sale agreement that protects you... You can do all the due diligence, but there are always exceptions."

So let's say you find a domain name you're interested in, you want to buy it, but the registrar has the registrant information locked. You're going to need to go through several hoops to find contact info and track the person down. But what if a cybercriminal has cheated the system? What if they've found a way to route an email to their own inbox or steal the real owner's identity?

There are too many bad actors out there who have figured out ways to cheat the system and can pass themselves off as the registrant. Before you know it, you've signed an agreement with them, wired money over—and then they are nowhere to be found and you still don't have the domain name. All the more reason to enlist the services of both a broker and attorney who can mitigate the risks. As a broker, I speak to attorneys every single week.

Brokers also have to become good detectives. I've even hired private investigators to help me out—tracking down addresses, employment history, mortgage information—any available information which can help us verify identities, ensure we're talking to the real owner of the domain, and help in making a reasonable, opening offer to the owner.

Beyond the various WHOIS databases, there are some other tools which buyers can use to help track down domain name registrants. DomainTools started out as a WHOIS database, but they realized that the data is what people want, so they began saving this info and tracking every domain name lookup. By doing so, they've built up a historical record of domain name registrations going back over twenty years. Domain IQ is a similar service, though a little cheaper and as of this printing Spaceship.com is another historical WHOIS service that's starting to catch on.

These services aid in verification because if you can see the same information for a domain name going back twenty years, there's higher confidence you're dealing with the true owner. Using Archive.org's Wayback machine is another helpful tool to be able to look up old web pages to hunt down info on the domain name owner.

HANDLING BAD ACTORS

Having an IP attorney is essential for handling bad actors because of how varied laws can be across states and nations. You need someone who knows how to follow the rules and regulations of each country, whether you're wanting to acquire a domain name owned by someone in another country—or you need to stop a bad actor.

One popular method employed by cybercriminals is to try to scam people by using a domain name similar to one they recognize. Someone might register a domain that is a misspelling of a well-known brand and then use it to reach out to people to try to get them to give up their info.

For example, let's say a cybercriminal sets up a domain name to impersonate the bank Wells Fargo, but they use WellsFarrgo.co. Then they go out and buy a list of emails and blast out some emails about an urgent account issue that needs attention. They can even make it look official, using the Wells Fargo logo in the body of the email. If someone isn't reading closely, they might fall for this and click on a phishing link in the email—or even get rerouted to another site for a money transfer and end up sending money to the bad actor.

In 2008, Verizon was awarded $33 million in a lawsuit against a cyber-squatter who had registered no less than 663 domain names infringing on their trademarks.[28] In 2024, they won $450K in another settlement against an individual who had registered nine domain names infringing on their trademark.[29]

I'll say that again... *$450,000 for nine domain names!* That's $50,000 per infringing domain name.

People are still trying to do this, so if you have such a domain name in your possession—then you better unload it fast. It's a ticking time bomb waiting to go off on you, depending on how litigious the trademark holder is.

Should you ever find yourself in a situation like Verizon, where someone is impersonating your brand, you have a legal basis for a subpoena. Contact a broker so you can get introduced to a licensed attorney who has experience in domain name and trademark infringement. Then the attorney can help you go after the bad actor since you have a legal basis for a forced acquisition of the domain name.

It's unusual for the bad actor to show up to court, of course. They don't want to get caught. Typically, they just let go of the domain name and go out to register more. But at least you'll have scared them off.

For these types of problems, ICANN created a process known as UDRP (also known as DNRP), the Uniform Domain Name Dispute Resolution Policy. This process allows legitimate domain name holders to go after bad actors. If that doesn't work and you're in the US, then IP and trade-mark issues are also dealt with by the US Federal Courts but it's much more expensive to go that route.

There's a potential for abuse with these systems, though. Sometimes people file frivolous cases because they think they should own the domain name, which ends up wasting everyone's time—and hurting their business.

Brent Oxley, the founder of HostGator, built a portfolio of high-value domain names. But in 2019, a civil suit was filed against him in an Indian court because an Indian broker claimed rights to some of the names in Oxley's portfolio. While it only cost the broker $11 to file the lawsuit, it resulted in the registrar locking Oxley's portfolio, which was worth upwards of $25 million.[30] Brent then turned around to launch his own lawsuit to get the domain names unlocked, which ended up getting escalated to international court and finally, a settlement.

Yet another reason to make sure you have an IP attorney involved from the get-go so you can get any agreements in writing and avoid such legal entanglements.

And for those who need ongoing brand protection—which is strongly encouraged—there are a number of well-established brand protection agencies to consider:

- Corporation Service Company (CSC)
- MarkMonitor
- Safebrands
- Brandsight (purchased by GoDaddy)
- Marksmen

All of these have extensive experience in the domain name industry, helping brands protect themselves from the bad actors out there who might attempt to infringe on their brand and other IP.

CONCLUSION

If you have additional questions about legal issues pertaining to domain names as intellectual property or cybersquatting, I'll cover some additional details in Chapter 15. But the best action you can take is to get connected with an IP attorney who specializes in domain names like David Weslow. Since laws and processes can change quickly, you want to make sure you're getting counsel from someone who is up-to-date rather than purely relying on information online, which can be easily outdated or misconstrued.

Throughout this first section of the book, our focus has been primarily on understanding domain names and the industry at large. As you move forward from here, we'll begin to look more into the nuances of domain names—how they operate as part of a brand (Section II), how to acquire them (Section III), how to sell a premium domain name (Section IV), and additional case studies (Section V).

SECTION II

DOMAINS AS MARKETING & BRANDING TOOLS

CHAPTER 7

HOW DOMAIN NAMES REPRESENT YOUR BRAND

WHEN YOU HEAR "Las Vegas," what do you think of? The bright lights of the strip? The fountains of Bellagio? Elvis (or his many impersonators) belting out "Viva Las Vegas" while dancing across the stage? Or—if you're feeling lucky—maybe hitting the floor for some blackjack and craps?

Whether you've visited "Sin City" or not, the name itself brings images to mind. That's the power of branding. And no doubt about it—the city of Las Vegas has its own brand. One worth billions.[31] So it should be no wonder that the name of the city itself holds strong marketing potential.

In 2005, LasVegas.com sold in a deal worth $90 million over the course of thirty-five years. Information from the SEC filing showed the agreement entailing a $12 million upfront payment with scaling monthly payments from the time of purchase until 2040.[32]

This puts the deal near the top of the charts for all-time domain valuations. A quick trip to LasVegas.com and you'll see why:

"Vacation your way at the all-new LasVegas.com. The top site for Las Vegas travel deals on hotels, shows, and things to do on your next Vegas vacation."[33]

Clearly, they want to be the one-stop shop for Vegas tourism, and have built their entire brand around the domain name. They know Las Vegas isn't going anywhere for a long time—and they'll continue to reap the financial benefits as long as they hold onto it.

The same could be said for Erik Allebest and Jay Severson who started up Chess.com in 2005, all from their love for the game itself. They wanted to create a home base for fellow lovers of chess—and today their website boasts over 100 million subscribers.[34]

That's the power of a strong domain name when it's connected to your brand. When a company is thinking about long-term growth and being recognized as the place for your service or niche, the price of the exact match domain name becomes a rounding error.

In our internet-driven world, brand and domain names are intricately wired together. Having a name that attracts attention is more important than ever before. So if you're thinking about the long-term marketing value of a new company or new product being launched by your business, it's never too soon to start thinking about how you'll connect the brand and domain together.

Owning the canonical search term domain name for your industry is the *best* money you'll ever spend on marketing.

BRAND & BRAND IDENTITY

The word "brand" gets thrown around a lot these days. Sometimes people use it to refer directly to the company who produced a product—"What brand of shoes do you like best? What brand of jeans are those?"

Online, it's impossible to escape discussions of "developing your personal brand," that is, your reputation as a businessperson. And if you're more historically-minded, then you can go all the way back 4,000 years to the Indus Valley where they first developed the practice of branding livestock.[35]

All of these are true, of course. Sometimes people make the mistake of thinking brand is just about a logo. But your brand is ultimately about being recognized, being noticed, and what you're *known* for. Granted, there is a heightened *visual* component to brand, but a fancy logo doesn't mean much if people don't know what you do—which brings us to brand identity.

When thinking about your brand, your identity is about the message you want to convey to consumers. It's about the story you want to tell—the meaning that lives *underneath* the words. So it's not unusual for this to be a more artistic and psychological process than it is utilitarian.

Remember the story of how I picked the name Brannans for my company? It's not a keyword-based brand name at all, but has a story associated with it—Samuel Brannan and the Gold Rush.

Likewise, Jeff Bezos was intentional in selecting the name "Amazon" back in 1994. Have you ever wondered why he didn't choose a name like "The Online Bookstore?" This would have been the more utilitarian name, but it has no personality, no story behind it. Plus, a name like that would have limited potential growth by confining him to the niche of books.

Originally, Bezos had picked the name "Cadabra, Inc." because he wanted people to think of buying a book online as a magical experience. But after several lawyers misheard the word as "cadaver," he realized it wasn't the best name—*not* the brand identity he wanted!

After a quick trip to the dictionary, he realized Amazon was a far more desirable name. It evoked the idea of adventure, of traveling to far-off lands—like you can do with a good book. Plus, it's much easier to spell than "Cadabra," which automatically makes it more valuable. In the long run, it's a much, much better brand name.[36]

Speaking of, Amazon is famous for successfully shifting their brand identity over the years. Even though Bezos started the company wanting it to be known as *the* online bookstore, the name Amazon could become an umbrella for unknown expansion. But as you already know, today's Amazon is known as the online shop for, well, pretty much anything. Their brand name hasn't changed—but the brand identity has evolved.

Their move in 2017 to acquire Whole Foods certainly raised some eyebrows, but looking at their trajectory, it made sense. As they became known more for retail beyond the online experience, having a brick-and-mortar point of contact with customers was an expansion of their identity rather than a total reshaping of it.

Contrast this with Colgate who, in 1982, tried to get into the food game. After all, they were already making products for the mouth—toothpaste, toothbrushes, floss—so why not expand into making the very items you're cleaning out of your mouth? They released a line of frozen products known as Colgate Kitchen Entrees. It was too much of a break in brand identity for consumers and failed to catch on, cutting into the company's profits.

And even Amazon has had its missteps. Remember the Fire Phone? Of course not. That's because they tried to get into the smartphone game too late and had no clear connection to their identity as an online retailer.[37]

Your brand is a form of communication, so before any change, you have to ask yourself, "Does my brand identity match what I'm trying to communicate to consumers?"

If you're rebranding to convey a shift in brand identity, then it's better to be *proactive*, not reactive.

Which is exactly why some companies choose to re-brand over time, so they can proactively align their purpose with their name.

For instance, Enterprise Rent-a-Car recently shifted their brand identity to become Enterprise Mobility, including purchasing EM.com to redirect to EnterpriseMobility.com. In short, they wanted to communicate, "Hey, we're not just about renting cars anymore—we're about many forms of mobility."

They communicate this on their website by saying, "Since day one, we've been inspired by a bold idea—creating better experience for how the world moves." They are expressing a simple idea: our name has changed but not our purpose.

And don't forget, Apple used to be Apple Computers. But as their offerings moved beyond strictly making computers, they dropped the "Computers" from their name. After all, today they are not only making computers, but smartphones, providing digital services like data storage and music, and even producing TV shows and movies. And we consumers let them get away with this because it's not inconsistent with their brand identity of innovation and making life easier for people.

Likewise, Dunkin' Donuts dropped "Donuts" from their name. On the surface, it sounds like a terrible business decision because at the time, the term Dunkin' was synonymous with donuts. But it proved to be stronger brand positioning since they had already started using the slogan, "America runs on Dunkin'," making the change a better way to capitalize on the rising popularity of their coffee. Think about it, when you think of Dunkin' right now, do you think about donuts, coffee, or both?

Unfortunately for Dunkin', at the time of writing, they haven't yet managed to acquire the exact match domain (EMD) name and are still relying on DunkinDonuts.com, which underscores why it's so important to have consistency between the domain name and your brand name. It packs more value than you might initially realize.

CONNECTION TO INTELLECTUAL PROPERTY AND TRADEMARK

If you skipped over Chapter 6, consider this a gentle nudge to go back and read it. Especially if you're someone with marketing on your brain, you're going to want to make sure the ideas you are generating are clear for you to use before you go and buy that domain name.

As the internet grows, it becomes easier to infringe on someone else's intellectual property and trademark, even if it wasn't your intention. You don't want to end up in a lawsuit and being forced to give up the name you've built your entire brand around.

Beyond the legal costs, this is often enough to damage a business because you are stripped of your identity. Some customers may abandon you because of the name change, or because they make an assumption that the lawsuit means your company is unscrupulous—even if you're not. Plus, the cost of rebranding, from selecting a new domain to reprinting all of your materials, updating legal filings . . . it all adds up fast.

But to think more positively about this topic, recognize that the brand name you select has an inestimable value to your long-term success. Your name is intellectual property and deserves protection. Seriously consider getting the trademark as proactive protection from bad actors down the road. Corporations are fantastic at thinking this way—small startups, less so.

While brokers like myself will always defer you to speak with a trademark and IP attorney, the fact is, we've dealt with so many situations that we can at the very least help get you moving in the right direction. We can help you think of the potential pitfalls you can't see when you're only focused on the name you want and you're not looking around to see if anyone else is already using it.

For instance, do you know about the Apple vs. Apple case?

As brilliant as he was, it's questionable whether Steve Jobs checked about potential problems with the name "Apple." Over the course of thirty years, there was an ongoing legal battle between Apple Corps and Apple Inc.

If you haven't heard of Apple Corps Limited, you know their work— they were started in January 1968 by The Beatles as a conglomerate, including Apple Records as the "core," if you'll pardon the pun. But they also spun off other companies stemming from The Beatles brand, including electronics, publishing, and retail.

Starting to see the problem?

During the lengthy disputes, Apple Inc. has had to pay multiple settlements to Apple Corps—including a payout of $27 million in 1991. Part of this agreement barred Apple Inc. from distributing music. But in 1991, the idea of Apple Inc. being in the music business was not a concern whatsoever. Whoops!

Most of us didn't know this was happening, but music lovers noticed something when iTunes launched in 2001—you couldn't buy any songs by The Beatles. This seemed like a massive oversight to many music fans, but it wasn't. It was all about IP and trademark. In an article released at the time of the settlement, Ringo was quoted as saying, "I am particularly glad to no longer be asked when the Beatles are coming to iTunes."[38]

When the dispute was settled on February 5, 2007, it was agreed that all "Apple" trademarks would move under Apple Inc. to the tune of $500 million. Talk about the value of a name!

Your name could very well end up being the most valuable asset you own, so you better put a ton of thought and research into it! In the next chapter, that's where we're headed—the marketing value of your domain name and some best practices you need to know.

CHAPTER 8

MARKETING VALUE OF A DOMAIN NAME

YOU MIGHT REMEMBER in Chapter 1, we talked about how people used to try to game Google with keyword-based domain names. The example used there was of someone buying a domain like "BestBakeryAtlanta.com." But after their Panda and Penguin updates, this is no longer an issue—which is good, because too many people were buying keyword-based domain names solely for the traffic but without any relevant content.

However, that's not to say keywords don't play a role in how you think about your brand. A strong keyword domain with relevant content can absolutely pay off. Look no further than Tiff's Treats.

Tiffany and Leon Chen met as students at UT in Austin, Texas. According to their own website, Tiff stood up Leon on a date and as an apology, made some cookies and personally delivered them to him. After a bite, he convinced her to start a business, which turned into Tiff's Treats.

What sets them apart from every other bakery is their delivery. They know the power of a warm, fresh-from-the-oven cookie. After all, that apology helped lead to them becoming partners in both business and life. They've set up a system which keeps the cookies warm on the way to their destination so that when they arrive, it's like they were just taken out of the oven.

The best marketing is word-of-mouth marketing. But you can't count on everyone remembering your name after only one taste. One of the smartest moves they ever made for their business was to buy the domain CookieDelivery.com. In fact, at the time of writing, if you type in "TiffsTreats.com," it will redirect you there.

They knew people might not remember Tiff, but they would remember "cookie delivery," so with that domain name under their control, they could also organically wield search results for "cookie delivery." Twenty-five years on, Tiff and Leon are still married, two kids, plus ninety-two stores across nine states with over 1700 employees.[39]

When your brand becomes known as the go-to for a niche, you not only get the power of word-of-mouth, but you also get the power of Google.

From my experience, there are two ways you can leverage the marketing value of a domain name:

1. Exact Match
2. Branding Power

So let's take a closer look at both of these and you can see what makes the most sense for your company.

EXACT MATCH

Exact match domain names are pretty easy to understand. It comes down to the specific product or service you want to be known for. Tiff's Treats having "CookieDelivery.com" is one example, but it's not as powerful as having the one-word match.

For instance, a few years ago, I bought Batteries.com. If you're in the battery power business, you *can't* find a better domain. You want the person searching for a battery to come find you and your service.

I used to own Cheesecake.com. When someone goes to Google and starts typing in "cheesecake," there could be a number of reasons why. Maybe they are wanting to find a cheesecake recipe. Maybe they are actually searching for a nearby Cheesecake Factory. Or maybe they are looking for a ready-made cheesecake to have delivered for an upcoming event.

I focused on the third group—people who were searching for the ready-made cheesecake that could be shipped anywhere in the US as a gift. Now, that's not to say it's a bust if traffic comes from some of those other queries. For instance, the person searching for a cheesecake recipe could get directed to their site and realize, "You know what, I don't have time to make a cheesecake—I'm just going to order one better than what I could make myself."

Either way, when you own the exact match, it automatically drives traffic and increases chances of converting to a sale. You are no longer just *a* service...you become *the* service. So the downside is it does put an extra burden on your shoulders—you've got to be able to deliver on the expectation or else it will hurt your brand.

A client of mine who falls into this camp is Lawn.com, which provides lawn care and landscaping services for homeowners and property managers. It doesn't take any clever explanation *why* they would want a domain like Lawn.com. When it went up for public auction, they brought me in to help them get it.

When you own the SLD that's a one-word .COM match, it lends a *massive* amount of customer credibility. You can't always put a price on that—though we certainly try our best. Simply put, people remember a name like Lawn.com. it automatically leads people to believe you're the expert in your field. It's insane how much people trust a company based on this one factor, leading bounce rates to go down and sales conversion rates to go up.

But what if you already have an existing brand or name in mind? How do you leverage branding power through a domain name?

BRAND MESSAGE

Many of the most powerful brand strategies are based around words which have no direct connection to the service itself but are chosen to communicate a message. These are often powerful one-word SLDs like colors, seasons, animals, and so on. My own company's name falls underneath this category since it is neither my name or directly describes my service.

For instance, with colors, you could think of RED digital cameras or Purple Mattress. For both companies, the name is more about the branding potential—the factor of memorability and standing out in a crowded market. For RED, it's the message of a powerful cinematic experience, symbolized by the "red carpet." For Purple, it's purely about being *different.*

When Purple first started, they didn't have Purple.com but were using OnPurple.com. According to the SEC filing, it cost them $900K in 2017 to acquire the one-word Purple.[40] No doubt acquiring the one-word brand name match was about long-term branding power—and it was a move which helped make them a recognizable, household brand.

According to the article, the previous owner wasn't even trying to sell the domain name—but simply got an offer they couldn't refuse. This is yet another reason underscoring why you need a good broker. Just because a name isn't "for sale" doesn't mean you can't get it to boost your branding power.

I can't put it any better than what domain name journalist James Iles says in his 2021 article about Purple's name acquisition:

> "At a certain point, it can become damaging for brands *not* to control their exact match .COM domain. For the sake of $900,000, would a company with a $1.1 billion valuation risk allowing its exact match .COM domain to be sold to another company looking to brand around the name? Purple mattresses are now stocked in stores across the U.S., but Purple's website remains the go-to for most Purple customers."[41]

In short, even if you reach a point where other people are carrying and selling your product for you, it still makes good business sense to own the .COM match for your brand.

Plenty of other examples abound. For animals, you might think of Elephant.com, which is owned by Elephant insurance. They know how much people love elephants, known for their strength, intelligence, and compassion—qualities they want to communicate to their customers. Or the athletic wear company Puma, whose name evokes speed and prowess. All of these fall under the category of branding power, not literal matches for what they *do*, but rather the message they want to send.

Abbreviations can also fall under this category. When people started using the abbreviation "FB" for Facebook, it became prudent for them to acquire FB.com even though it was costly for them to do so. They had a brand reputation to protect and the cost of acquisition was certainly less than having to deal with not owning it. When Kylie Jenner launched her fashion brand KHY, it made sense for her to buy KHY.com,[42] and so on.

If you're in marketing for a corporation—or even a small business—you have to be on the front line of the domain name decision. If you are a CMO or report to one, you have to make sure the domain name is tied into the messaging of the company. First, for the consistency and reputation, but also for the sheer value of the asset.

Remember, domain names are not always just about the company's website or name, but also about increasing visibility for a product or service. The product might "live" on your website, but having its own assigned domain gives it an extra SEO boost and additional brand credibility. So when it comes to product positioning for an already-established brand or company, these concepts still hold true.

MARKETING TESTS

In all my years of brokering, I've adopted some rules and tests around the marketability power of a brand name. Some of these I've learned directly from entrepreneurs who have explained their thought process—others have been learned by reading books on subjects I'm interested in. While this is by no means a foolproof method for marketing success, you can definitely use it as a guide when weighing options for brand names.

MEMORABILITY—AKA, THE THIRD-GRADER RULE

Marketing value is rooted in memorability. If you make a great product but no one remembers who *you* are, then you've failed. How will they find your product? Or what if they end up with your direct competitor?

Most of the companies I've mentioned in this chapter easily pass the test of being memorable. Possibly the one exception here is KHY, but if you've already got the platform of someone like Kylie Jenner, then you might have some leverage to bypass this rule. For the rest of us, memorability is key.

You can better guarantee memorability by following this checklist:

- Is it easy to pronounce?
- Is it easy to spell?
- Is it a short word in English?

Personally, I follow "The Third-Grader Rule"—If a third-grader can recite the name back to you, then you've passed the test of memorability.

Memorability is a major factor for why companies choose to upgrade from a less-desirable domain to a premium one. For many brands, they might be starting out in a garage. I'm currently consulting a client on this very issue. They started out as a scrappy startup, became a TechStars alum, and now they're looking into acquiring the exact-match .COM for their brand.

Once again, I have to return to my favorite sermon of why you need .COM over an alternative like .XYZ or .CO. Learn from Overstock's mistake when they tried to switch to O.co. That one move led them to a staggering (and costly) failure rate of over 60 percent of visitors typing in O.com instead. MeetMe saw a very similar problem when they tried to use Meet.me as their domain. Eventually, this forced them to acquire MeetMe.com to save the brand.

Which domain name do you think MeetMe knows is more valuable? Type in *Meet.me* to see the answer.

ROAD TESTED—AKA, THE URBAN DICTIONARY RULE

Just like you would with a car, first you've got to make a list of what names you're considering. Brainstorm twenty to thirty names with variations like plurals and synonym terms, in the same way you would make a list of potential cars with varying features like color, seat coverings, and so on.

But next, you better take your domain name ideas for a road test. Once you've brainstormed about twenty or thirty ideas, you need to start filtering them with your legal team and marketing team. They can help you with crossing off options that would violate someone else's trademark and save you the legal hassle.

But they can also catch bigger problems you maybe didn't think of, such as if a term has a negative or illicit connotation. To keep things PG here, I won't go into details, but I once knew of a situation regarding a name which could also have a sexual meaning based on the spelling. While plenty of people use the term for other reasons, the top prospect walked away—they didn't want to deal with the potential negative PR or jokes at the company's expense.

The same can be said for street names of illicit drugs. While there's nothing inherently wrong with the name "Molly," you might think twice about acquiring it when you know it's a nickname for ecstasy or MDMA.

Exactly why I call this one "The Urban Dictionary Rule." If it's got a double meaning in Urban Dictionary, then you want to at least be cautious. It shouldn't necessarily lead to an immediate disqualification, but it's always better to be aware before you have a problem.

Beyond the possible PR nightmares, another reason to road test connotations is to clarify your message. A few years ago, WeightWatchers rebranded their messaging. While their products and services still use the name "WeightWatchers," they changed their official company name to WW International, shifting their focus to center around wellness, not just weight. They also rebranded with the ultra-premium domain name, WW.com.

These considerations make you tap into the "Why" aspect of your brand's marketing strategy—what is the purpose you want to be known for? You convey your purpose through words—therefore, the words hold great value.

SOUND TESTED—AKA, THE RADIO TEST

Does your domain name prospect pass the verbal test when said aloud? This is what branding pros often call "The Radio Test." If your brand has no visual cues for the consumer because it's being said over the radio or a phone call, would the listener know how to spell it?

Homonyms consistently fail this test. Is it Meat.com? Or Meet.com? Is it Reed.com? Or Read.com? You can see—or rather, *hear* the problem. Difficult to pronounce words also fail the test, such as "rural" or "squirrel." Naming your company or product "Rural Squirrel" would be like signing your brand's death certificate—though it might make a cute children's book.

On this note, also consider if a word can be pronounced more than one way. Examples would be words like "drawer," "oil," "syrup," and "caramel." Or take a word like "picture," which many Americans pronounce as "pitcher." This could easily lead to more misunderstandings around your brand: Do you mean pitcher like a receptacle for liquid? Or pitcher like in baseball?

Also, don't overlook the power of alliteration. Memorability loves alliteration and I find it's an under-utilized aspect of branding. When it's done well, it can do wonders. Best Buy, Coca-Cola, Krispy Kreme, and so on. Just keep in mind that even the best alliteration in your SLD cannot overpower the disadvantage of a second-rate TLD like .CO or .XYZ. People will still type in .COM most of the time.

COGNITIVE BIAS—AKA, THE ANCHORING EFFECT

In general, I'm wary about online valuation tools as they can often be wrong. So this test is more of a warning than anything else. If you're trying to price out a potential domain name by using an online valuation tool, don't be surprised if the owner ends up asking for more than what the tool told you.

This is what's called "The Anchoring Effect." It's the reason most car dealerships slap a pricing sticker on the window. They know that when most people see the number, it gets anchored in the mind and creates a cognitive bias that, "This must be the *absolute* value because it's what the sticker says." It's a tactic designed to discourage customers from haggling—and it often works.

Similarly, I've had people come to me wanting to acquire a domain name owned by someone else and say, "I think we should only offer $4000 because the valuation tool said it's worth $3500. They can't say no to us if we're offering over valuation, right?"

Don't count on it.

This type of cognitive bias works against us the most when it's a name that's *not* for sale—even when it's not in active use. Corporations or high net worth individuals place an entirely different value on a domain, especially when it's tied to any intellectual property, email servers, or systems still associated with the domain.

This holds true for personal names as well. People are going to assign their own value to what their name is worth to them. And as a bonus tip, I've noticed male domain name owners tend to place a higher value on their name than female domain name owners do. We won't get into the societal implications of this trend in this book, though—I'll let a sociologist handle that one.

When it comes to valuation tools, potential buyers overlook the fact these are algorithm-based and therefore, they are still guesses at best. The value of a domain name is truly set more by the seller than anyone else at the table. So remember, if they live in a $10 million home and have a yacht down at the marina, they won't care two cents what the valuation tool says. Even if they don't have such great assets, but maybe they are looking to wipe out some debt or start a new venture, the dollar sign in their mind holds far more value to them than any appraisal you come to the table with.

Which leads us to the final test to apply...

AFFORDABILITY—AKA, THE BUDGET TEST

Sometimes your budget is the deciding factor for a domain name. When you're a scrappy startup, you simply may not be able to afford the name you want yet. You're in good company, though. Many of today's top brands started out with second-choice domain names simply because the name they truly wanted wasn't available—and acquiring it didn't pass their budget test.

Ideally, you find the SLD exact match .COM for your brand and it's 100 percent available at a price you can afford to pay. Just keep in mind that the better names are going to require more significant investments.

If you can't fully trust a valuation tool, then what can you trust? Once more, this is where knowing a domain name broker is going to be helpful. Not only can we help you negotiate a more realistic price for the domain name you want, but we can also explore options to pass your budget test.

Sometimes you don't have to pay for the name outright. You could be able to finance it over time—or put cash down for part of it and supplement the rest for stock options in your company. And while a domain name is being financed, you should be able to use it, too. We've helped a lot of clients get their top choice domain name with owner financed domain transactions.

As we'll look at soon, though, the best practice is to buy your exact match as soon as possible. It will only become more expensive over time—and someone else could get it first, forcing you to change your entire brand strategy. The more of these tests that a domain name can pass, the higher its marketing value to you (and others).

The next question we have to tackle, though, is how do you settle on the name? With so many words in the English language (SLDs) mixed with the various TLDs available, you have limitless options. The tests here should help you whittle down your list, but now we need to turn to the process of landing on a name which enhances your visibility—and your value.

CHAPTER 9

ASSESSING DOMAIN NAMES

A S A HEAD'S up, the focus of this chapter is going to be on assessing domain names while you are still in the naming process of your company. However, most of the advice here also applies if you are either rebranding and renaming a company—or if your company is branching out with a new brand, label, or offering.

But first, I want you to consider a business concept with me: Discovery.

In sales, discovery is the process of figuring out what your customer actually needs rather than assuming. It requires skills in asking good questions, true listening, and knowing your product or service so well you can assess quickly how to position your offering as the solution to your prospect's need.

As a domain name broker, we follow a similar process. Whether we are helping a client buy or sell a domain name, we have to discover *who* is the best match, where it will gain the highest value based on the marketing appeal.

You could consider this "The Discovery Test," the final filter you use when assessing domain names for your brand. How does it work?

My favorite non-English word is the French term *Juilletistes*. While we have no English equivalent, it refers to people in France who take the entire month of July off to go on a "Grand Vacation." (Of course, they also generally have one to three more weeks of vacation a year outside of July.)

You'll also find people in France who are *Aoûtiens*, meaning they take a month off in August instead. If this was a practice in the US, we might call them "Julyists" or "Augustians."

As a callback to the last chapter, let's say I meet with an executive from Casino de Monte-Carlo in Monaco. They say they're looking to add a new domain name for marketing purposes. In the discovery process, I would ask, "Who are you trying to reach?"

"The French. We need them to trade in casinos in France for ours in Monaco."

When they say this, my alarm bells will go off. "Then you should consider *Juilletistes.com*," I'll say.

For most people, I'd never recommend this. Why? Because neither word passes many of the tests and rules from the last chapter. But oftentimes, assessing the true marketing value of a domain name is about knowing your *audience*. Those terms will hold the highest marketing value for the gambling industry in a way that would be worthless for a bakery or a pet goods retailer.

It's never enough to simply have a catchy one-word domain name. You have to know your market well enough to understand who you want to attract. You'll find plenty of marketing reasons to have a domain name that *doesn't* match your company name.

Keep this in mind as we apply the tests and rules from Chapter 8.

CHICKEN OR THE EGG?

Founders and entrepreneurs often find themselves in a chicken-or-egg scenario when they are first starting out:

What should come first? The company name? Or the domain name?

You can probably guess my bias. If you're still in the early stages of developing your company, then go with the domain name first. Assuming the name is available at a price you can pay, you'll want to snap it up before someone else does.

If on the other hand, it's not available and it's a good name with a high discoverability factor, be aware that this will raise the price the seller asks for. It's a simple case of supply and demand—once the demand is there, the price will go up. Especially on a limited, unique asset like a domain name.

So as much as possible, you want to see if you can pick up the domain name before you name the company, release a product, or do any other kind of press release. Otherwise, you're going to be sending your traffic to whoever owns the exact-match .COM.

Generally, you're better off acquiring the domain name first, then naming the company, and then registering the company before you start using the name.

For instance, in Chapter 7, I gave the example of Amazon and how Jeff Bezos originally formed the company under the name "Cadabra." But he had to pivot to Amazon. Granted, he did this in 1994 when it was much easier to acquire a premium word like "amazon." You won't find it nearly so simple nowadays.

There's a couple of other factors to consider, though: Discoverability and Availability.

DISCOVERABILITY

The discoverability factor plays a massive role in marketing as you already saw in the opening example. But let's imagine for a second that you're starting an accounting firm. You may already know you need to stick to standard industry practice and have your firm named after yourself. But maybe you decide you want to focus on accounting *only* for construction companies. You want to be known as *the* accounting firm for construction.

Knowing who you're trying to reach, you might then decide it's prudent to brainstorm some domain names with some SEO power behind them:

ConstructionAccountant.com
ConstructionAccounting.com
ContractorAccounting.com

And so on. Acquiring the domain name with a high discoverability factor can be a major asset to your business in the long run. But first, you'll need to find out if it's available—and if not, whether it can be *made* available.

AVAILABILITY

Once you've brainstormed your discoverability domain ideas, you'll start to do your homework to find out which names might be available—and what the asking price is. Yes, you'll also buy a domain name that's an exact match for your company name, but you'll want to make sure any keyword-based domains acquired for SEO purposes reroute traffic to your website.

Don't be surprised if the name you're after is already registered, even if it's not being actively used. If the name you pick passes the marketing tests I mentioned in Chapter 8, it *is* going to be registered. That's not a guess. There are over 367,000,000 registered domain names at this point.

> ALL of the good domains are already registered, and the really good domains have been registered for over twenty years.

Sometimes the registrant simply does not want to part ways with the domain because they have future plans for it. If availability is blocking your way, you might have to go with another domain name out of sheer necessity.

Plenty of examples exist of this, especially among startups. Famously, Facebook started as TheFacebook.com. And I previously mentioned the new soda brand Poppi, which started out with the SLD of "DrinkPoppi" since they could not acquire the exact match .COM. As you can imagine, this necessitates more ad spend on their part to make sure they still show up at the top of search results.

Many scrappy startups follow the same example, putting words like "the," "get," or "buy" in their SLD so that they can at least have the optimal TLD of .COM. Which brings us back to keywords. This is what I recommend if the budget is tight at this point but you are already set on a brand name.

LEVERAGING KEYWORD DOMAINS

Remember, Google no longer favors you just because you have a keyword domain—but it can make great brand sense to use one, especially if it's highly discoverable and available. It'll just need to be developed and the SEO will come.

In the last chapter, I mentioned Cheesecake.com. Before Panda and Penguin, the domain name BuyCheesecake.com would have been incredibly useful to own as well because people that search the keyword, "buy cheesecake online," have an incredibly high conversion rate—sometimes it's as high as 80 percent.

But what about now? If you're starting a business on this side of the algorithm change, when does it make sense to also own a keyword domain?

A few years ago, I helped Gourmet Gift Baskets with acquiring a keyword-based domain as part of their marketing strategy. First, consider the fact they have been featured twice on Oprah and also hold two Guinness World Book records. This goes to show that "being featured" in media is not always the best way to stay relevant in the market. People move on to the next episode, the next headline, and you're yesterday's news.

The keyword domain that Gourmet Gift Baskets wanted to acquire was GiftBaskets.com, knowing that people are more likely to type in "gift baskets" than they are to type "gourmet gift baskets." It's simple math— more website visitors mean more sales.

Having a keyword domain can also help separate you from another company with a similar name, especially if you're not able to get the exact match away from them. For example, there are two companies named Graco. The first is an industrial fluids and solutions company— the second is the better-known baby accessory company.

But guess which one owns Graco.com?

The fluid company. And my guess is they're not letting it go.

So to help distinguish themselves, it made sense for the other Graco to leverage a keyword domain—GracoBaby.com. It's not ideal, but it's better than trying to use an alternative TLD like .CO or .NET, which would certainly lead to further marketing problems.

Believe me, I know this can be a confusing arena. But when it comes to marketing, few decisions you make with marketing are more important than *your name*. In the next section of the book, we'll explore more about the buying and acquisition process once you have your name and strategy set. But first, let's cover some of the most frequently asked questions I get about domain name branding and marketing.

BRAND-RELATED FAQS

Let's just be honest and get the big one out of the way:

Q: How much is the brand name going to cost?

A: The frustrating part of this entire conversation is the cost depends.

It depends on the name and who has it. If someone holding it needs liquidity, they might let it go for less than someone who doesn't need the money. Exactly why you should enlist a broker early on in the process to help you determine if a name is worth chasing after.

I never want to anchor people to a number because of cognitive bias. I've seen the resulting sticker shock too many times. You should always find out what the price is going to be. If you find out the price tag is too rich for your budget, it frees you up to pursue other names before you have to go rename your company and rework your entire strategy.

Q: How long will it take me to acquire the brand name I want?

A: Once again, it depends. However, we have a safe range we can work with based on experience. If you're acquiring an inactive name from a corporation, be aware they will take the longest. Many people will have to weigh in on the decision, starting with whether they even want to entertain an offer.

For example, I've seen Verizon take two years to decide to part with a domain they owned. This time was devoted to the process of untangling systems and data from the name being sold. After that, it took another year for us to get a price for the domain name. So, three years just to find out the price. Though these sorts of lengthy transactions are exceptions, they *do* happen, so you need to know that going in.

If you're buying from an individual, the process of getting a decision on whether or not to sell and getting a price typically goes faster. You might only be looking at a matter of weeks for a motivated seller. Even with a less motivated seller, you could still have the name within a couple of months, assuming you have a good broker worth their salt.

But on average, with a domain name that's not for sale and an unmotivated seller, you can expect the full transaction to take two to twelve months—so plan accordingly.

Q: If the exact match isn't available, is it better to just go with the keyword name or should we rethink our name entirely?

A: You could make a case for both. What I find helpful for this decision is to think of it like real estate. One time while walking in Huntington Beach, I noticed the properties from one block to the next were nearly identical in build. Yet when I priced them out, the properties two blocks away from the beach more expensive than the properties three blocks away. And those right up against the beach were the most expensive. In real estate, this has been summed up for years simply as, "Location. Location. Location."

A keyword-based domain using words like "buy" and "get" is like being three or four blocks away from the beach. You'll still get some traffic, but maybe not as much as you want. GracoBaby.com is an example of a keyword domain that's also like being two or three blocks away. It's still a very strong contender because it considers discoverability since they can't get the exact match.

I've never spoken to them, but Graco's reasoning is probably that they don't think that website visitors bring in sales since their products can be found in major retailers like Walmart and Target. If they needed web traffic, then it may be better to consider ponying up for the exact match that gets them closer to the beach, so to speak.

What they're still missing, though, is the brand signal that owning Graco.com sends. The trust factor would be higher for their products if they owned and used Graco.com over GracoBaby.com. They're already a $15 billion dollar company so making a large investment in Graco.com is like a rounding error on the books, even with a slight tick in market cap.

Ultimately, you should go with the brand name that gets you closer to the shore—whether it's a company or product name.

With Section III, we're going to move our focus even further into the realm of acquiring your desired domain name, especially when it's not publicly available on the marketplace. So if your question wasn't answered here, there's a good chance we'll cover it in the following chapters.

However, if you've still got questions related to the marketing value of domain names, I'm always happy to consult and at least help you get pointed in the right direction. You can reach out and schedule a consultation with me by visiting *brannans.com/contact/* and complete the form you'll find there.

SECTION III

BUYING
A DOMAIN NAME

CHAPTER 10

BUYING A NEW DOMAIN NAME

EVERYONE KNOWS CENTRAL Park in New York City. Not everyone knows who to thank for it—Frederick Law Olmstead. Hailing from Connecticut, Olmstead is now remembered as the father of landscape architecture here in the United States. For two decades, he traveled the world, including sailing for an entire year working in the China trade, a walking tour across Europe and the British Isles, and even across the US as a reporter for the *New York Times*.[43]

It was in 1858, though, when he and his design partner Calvert Vaux won a design competition for Central Park and began supervising its construction. For the next seven years, their lives were devoted to urban development as they were commissioned to design everything from cemeteries to private estates.[44]

A few years ago, I read a book about Olmstead where it had a great story of him persuading city officials across the country into buying up land to turn into parks. His premise was simple—If you don't buy the land now, it's only going to get more expensive later. Your constituents are paying taxes each year, so you'll end up costing the taxpayers even more money if you delay.

Olmstead was thinking not only years ahead but decades ahead as he helped establish parks and communities around the nation, including one near Atlanta, where I live.

In many ways, it echoes my own advice to those who are considering buying a domain name—Do it now. It will only get more expensive for you later on.

Originally, Central Park was budgeted as a $5 million project for the city, though the final tab came to $14 million. Even so, think about what it's worth today. For the past four decades, nearly $1 billion has been invested into Central Park which boasts upwards of forty-two million visitors a year.[45]

If your domain name is your digital real estate, then what are you willing to invest into it to ensure more visitors?

GENERAL STEPS

Some of what we cover here will repeat earlier information that was scattered across different chapters.

Generally speaking, I find three groups who are looking to buy a domain name:

1. Founders/Entrepreneurs: People who are launching a startup and need a name.
2. Existing Companies: Companies who need a new domain name for a new offering.
3. Venture Capital: Investment firms who are looking to add a domain name to one of their portfolio of companies as a strategic move.

More than likely, you can place yourself in one of these three groups—you're considering a name for a business idea, you work for a company who has tasked you with identifying a domain name as part of a marketing strategy, or you are part of a VC firm looking to strengthen traffic or branding for a company you are invested in.

For now, let's assume the domain name you're looking for is already listed for sale somewhere or it can simply be registered. In the next chapter, we'll focus on acquiring a domain name that isn't listed for sale.

1. CHECK AVAILABILITY

As discussed in Section II, you're going to want to make sure you have a list of domain names that align with your brand and that you've already cleared for availability, both in terms of the name and the trademark.

If you're looking at a name less than $10K, then one of the best places you can check availability is at GoDaddy. Chances are, you've already been there and done some playing around to see what names are available. The algorithm is robust enough, it can even help you with the brainstorming process by suggesting some alternative names if the first one you want isn't available. When it comes to domain names, GoDaddy is considered the default search engine for words in the same way Google is for pretty much everything else. (Although Chat.com is quickly becoming my default search engine.)

Of course, they are not the only registrar out there. Some other popular sites include:

- Namecheap
- IONOS
- Bluehost
- DreamHost
- Hover
- Hostinger
- Dynadot
- NameSilo

Ultimately, your decision comes down to the pricing you're looking for and any additional services you require, especially in terms of security. The last thing you want is going through the trouble of acquiring a domain name just to have someone steal it away from you.

2. PURCHASE THE DOMAIN NAME

Assuming the name you want is in your budget, you might as well go ahead and move it over to the cart. You might also decide on adding some additional services from the registrar, but this is totally up to you.

No matter what you end up paying, remember that your domain name is its own indefinitely lived, intangible asset. It may very well be your business's first piece of intellectual property (IP) and many businesses have discovered it ends up being the most valuable asset they have.

In the popular TV series *The Office*, you might recall Season 7, Episode 9 titled "WUPHF.com," where the plot revolved around the character

Ryan launching a social media startup called WUPHF which he ropes several of the other members of the office into investing in. However, as the company continues to hemorrhage money, it turns out the only thing of value is the domain name, which they end up selling off to cover their losses.

While this makes for a humorous plot, the scenario has happened in real life for companies when they are liquidating or merging. When Bed Bath & Beyond collapsed, it was reported that they sold their intellectual property and digital assets (which included their domain names) for $21.5 million to Overstock.[46]

3. SET SYSTEMS

If the registrar you buy from gives you the option to auto-renew your domain name registration each year, you should go ahead and do so. It's unfortunate when businesses fail to remember to renew the domain name and then someone else in the market—an investor or even a competitor—swoops in and buys the name away.

Because it's a near guarantee you that if you let a domain name lapse, you will have to cough up what *they* want for it to get it back. Otherwise, you're left facing the prospect of eating the cost of a *new* domain name and then having to rebrand everything. Plus, you'd need to track down customers to tell them your domain name is now different. You'll take a reputation hit.

But you also need a system for how the domain name will be managed. Ideally, you want it assigned to an email that more than one person has access to—just in case. We'll cover this in more detail later when discussing some of the major pitfalls corporations face with domain name management, but it still applies for startups.

Your business will inevitably change, including the people within it. So you don't want the domain name tied to just one person. If something happens to them, you could find yourself up a creek without a paddle. Create a corporate policy for how to manage the domain name, even if you're still small. It will serve you well later on.

BEST PRACTICES

It's not terribly complicated to register a domain name that's already available. Sometimes you might only be dropping $12 to $100 for your first entire year of registration, which is well worth the investment.

But to ensure you get the most out of the experience and that you don't create regret for yourself later on, then make sure you're also considering the following best practices:

#1: THERE'S NEVER GOING TO BE A CHEAPER TIME TO BUY A DOMAIN NAME THAN RIGHT NOW

Part of why Olmstead was so persuasive with city officials, especially in New York, was his ability to sell them on the long-term value of a city park. I'm paraphrasing, but he essentially said, "Look, if you build a great park, the property value around the park will become more desirable, and therefore, more valuable. As the property value goes up, so do the property taxes. The city will make more money in the long run, so this is actually an investment."

It all boiled down to dirt. Olmstead's point was that no more dirt was being made—especially on an island like Manhattan—which would only create more demand for the dirt already there. Unlike dirt, more domain names are being made—however, great ones are becoming *much* more scarce.

Your domain name is an investment. Sometimes new business owners can balk at the price of a domain name, especially if they're strapped for cash and the name they want is in the 4-figure range—or higher. But remember—the price is only going to go up from here.

#2. NEVER UNDERESTIMATE THE POWER OF A ONE-WORD OR LAST NAME .COM

If you need a refresher on why having a .COM in your domain is the best practice compared to alternate TLDs, then you may want to refer back to the biggest myths covered in Chapter 1. But in short, having a short, easy-to-remember, easy-to-spell one-word .COM is one of the most powerful, forward-thinking moves you can make for your brand.

The English language has around 170,000 words, but once you eradicate all the difficult-to-spell words like *onomatopoeia* and *vociferous*, you're left with a much smaller slate to choose from.

And as tempting as it might be to grab the lower-priced .CO, don't forget about human psychology. Most people will still end up typing in ".COM" on their keyboard, which means you'll be sending your traffic to the wrong place—and probably confusing your would-be customers.

We'll touch on this more in the next chapter for what to do when your one-word .COM is already registered by someone else, but it's a mistake to underestimate how much power a one-word or last name SLD paired with a .COM has for a brand. A quick scan of the Fortune 500 reveals plenty of one-word or last name .COM domains:

- Amazon
- Apple
- Oracle
- Chevron
- Alphabet
- Delta
- Target
- Ford
- McKesson
- Dell
- Marriott

While it's true many of these companies existed before the age of the internet, this fact only proves just how powerful a single-word or single-name SLD name is. And while some companies can get away with creating their own, unique spelling—such as Google (an intentional misspelling of googol) or Microsoft (a combination of the words "microcomputer" and "software"), these are outliers rather than the conventional wisdom you should follow. With both of these, they follow the Third-Grader Rule—they're easy to spell and pronounce, making them more memorable.

If you think you don't need the .COM for your brand, you're only kidding yourself. But we'll cover why in Best Practice #4. At the very least, you need to take a step back, discuss the issue with people in your circle—people you trust who understand marketing, branding, domain names, and most importantly, *conversion rates*. The evidence is that companies who go after the one-word .COM end up doing better.

#3: DON'T NEGLECT TO DO YOUR DUE DILIGENCE

In Section II, I touched on the importance of ensuring you're not accidentally violating someone's trademark. It's incredibly easy, quick, and cheap to check with the US Trademark and Patent Office—as well as easy, quick, and cheap to check name availability on GoDaddy.

You also don't want to end up as an accidental cybersquatter. If someone else has a trademark or protected term and they think your name is too similar to theirs, then you might end up getting a cease and desist letter. So before you buy the domain name or pick your company name, you should consult an attorney to help you identify any potential conflict.

A few years ago, I worked with a client who ran into a trademark issue with their name, though there was certainly no malice or ill intent on their part. They had bought the domain KingOfPop.com because one of their products was *popcorn* and they had been unable to secure "KingOfPopcorn.com." But this put a target on their backs from none other than the Michael Jackson estate, since he was widely known as "the King of Pop."[47]

As the broker of the domain name, I ended up being deposed and had to go talk to a bunch of attorneys who looked very serious and expensive. In the end, the two sides were able to reach a settlement over the issue, with Michael Jackson's estate acquiring KingOfPop.com as a result.[48] While this case may seem like an outlier, it underscores how easy it can be to step on someone else's IP and trademark toes. (Note: KingOfPops.com isn't owned by the Michael Jackson estate but KingOfPop.com now redirects to MichaelJackson.com.)

It's worth looking into professional liability insurance because there is a specific clause in E&O insurance (errors and omissions), where you can get a rider to protect you in case of unintentional trademark and IP issues. A friend of mine had this clause in his insurance and when he ran into a similar problem, the insurance paid the lion's share of the legal fees that resulted.

A common trait for young, successful entrepreneurs is their admirable and unshakeable belief in themselves. If they think they can do something, they'll do it—and they often succeed because of their ignorance of failure. Look no further than Elon Musk. He's consistently found success by doing what people told him he couldn't do—first with PayPal, then Tesla, and even with SpaceX. Everyone told him his rockets would *explode* and the business would *implode*. So what did he do? Go out and teach himself engineering and rocket science.

But there's a difference between a can-do spirit and simply *not* doing your homework. Ignoring another brand's IP and trademark is an oversight which will raise a red flag and could cost you hundreds of thousands. Remember the Apple vs. Apple story in Chapter 8? Better you spend $5K to 10K up front to make sure you're not infringing on anyone's trademark or IP.

Also, if you're going to have multiple locations across states, you are going to have to follow each state's business laws—not just those of your headquarters. Start by visiting the Trademark Search tool on the US Patent and Trademark Office website.[49] If you see a ton of dead and abandoned trademark names, let that be a red flag to you—it could mean that the trademark owner is litigious. And always ask an attorney for legal advice before you do anything.

Just like with your domain name, you want to set systems for renewing your trademark. A famous example in the US is that of the Duracell Bunny. Duracell got sloppy and let their bunny trademark expire—so Energizer swooped in and trademarked their own bunny to use in their ads. It was a super-smart move by them and today, many people in the US don't even realize Duracell started the bunny trend. If you go over to other countries, though, you'll still see the Duracell Bunny used in ads overseas because they didn't let their trademark lapse there.

Speaking of, if you intend for your business to be international, you're going to find different trademark and IP rules in place across countries. So depending on where you're scaling your business, you might end up needing more than the US trademark search. And you might also need to look into whether the international domain names are clear for you to use.

For instance, if you plan on doing business in Canada, you should really look at getting your domain name (SLD) with the .CA (ccTLD). These tend to convert better for sales than .COM because Canadian customers like to buy Canadian.

You'll also want to do a search for any trademark you want to own in another country. When Burger King wanted to expand into Australia, they ran into a problem—an Australian burger chain had already grabbed the name "Burger King," and there was nothing the corporation could do to try to enforce the US trademark. So in Australia, they had to settle for a new name—Hungry Jack's. Same logo, same burgers, but different name.

#4. DON'T SPREAD YOUR DOMAINS ACROSS DIFFERENT REGISTRARS.

If you want to prevent losing your domain names, a simple best practice for protecting them is to keep them all at the same registrar. Even though GoDaddy is the biggest, there are lots of registrars out there—and if you end up having fifty domain names scattered across multiple registrars, it's only a matter of time before one of them lapses.

It is possible to move a registration from one registrar to another, so if you find yourself with scattered domains, you can fix the problem. Brand protection agencies (BPAs) like MarkMonitor and CSC provide such services for securing and managing domain names. Get them all under the same registrar, under "one roof," so to speak.

This should go side-by-side with the step mentioned earlier about setting systems for your domain name management. Once you have all your domain names moved under your registrar of choice, you will automatically be more secure—plus, you'll be saving yourself from future headaches.

#5. DON'T DELAY ON THE PREMIUM DOMAIN NAME

When you're first starting out, it makes sense you may not have the cash for the premium domain name of your dreams. The problem I've seen with companies, though, is they become complacent with their second-rate name. They look at their numbers and say, "We're growing and sales are strong, so why switch things up?"

It's a fair question to ask. When things are going well, it's easy to justify staying the course, even if you've got the cash now for the premium domain name. The thinking is "If it ain't broke, don't fix it." But just because something isn't broken doesn't mean it can't be better.

Complacency is the first sign of a company in decline. The best way to avoid complacency is to remain active—and this includes getting the premium domain name.

For starters, the premium one-word .COM domain name is automatically going to drive higher traffic for the reasons I mentioned before. When Jim Campbell, the founder of Honeymoons.com, first started the business, they had to use the second-choice HoneymoonGoals.com. In July of 2023, they finally acquired Honeymoons.com for mid-six figures.

Was it worth the investment? You bet.

According to Jim, the change led to "a 7x increase in traffic and a 10x increase in revenue."[50] Now imagine if they had been able to start out with the premium domain name—how could it have accelerated their growth earlier on?

CONCLUSION

In the case of Honeymoons.com, it's what we call a "domain name upgrade." This is different from acquiring a completely brand new name, but the same principles apply. Still, there are some nuances to acquiring an existing domain name—especially if it's a premium name.

So what do you do when someone else has the domain name you want? Where can you go "shopping" for a premium domain name? When is the right time to bring in a broker to help with the acquisition? And what steps do you need to take to acquire it? Let's take a closer look now at the process and best practices for acquiring an existing domain name.

CHAPTER 11

ACQUIRING AN EXISTING DOMAIN NAME

I N THE ANCIENT days of the internet—October 2, 1997, to be exact—a lady named Frida in Norway registered the domain name Frida.com so she could use it for email. And that's mainly all she ever did with the domain name—used it to communicate over email.

Fast forward seventeen years later, and a company called Frida Baby was born into the world.

You might know them for the NoseFrida—a device that allows parents to suction the snot out of their baby's nose. They've built a thriving business and their products help thousands of parents around the world.

They started out with the domain name FridaBaby.com since this was officially their name, but it wasn't particularly powerful for driving traffic. They wanted to upgrade to the one-word .COM, the premium name Frida.com.

When they approached me about trying to acquire the name, we started with our due diligence to make sure the name checked off all the boxes they wanted. Most importantly, we wanted to make sure we were reaching out to the correct person since there are plenty of scammers out there who will claim to own a domain name and then run off with your money.

By researching the ownership history of the name, I was able to help them confirm we had the right person to reach out to. I reached out to make initial contact and received a polite, "The name is not for sale, thank you."

Some might be discouraged by this, but I've been doing this long enough to know it was a good sign she was responding. It's a really bad sign when you get no response. Over a period of several months, we maintained steady correspondence, helping her to start emotionally detaching from the domain name.

See, the owner wasn't initially interested in any kind of monetary gain from selling the name. A knee-jerk response of "no thanks" has little to do with dollars but usually everything to do with identity.

First, I had to let her know how serious the company was—until eventually it was safe to ask, "If you were to come up with a number for my client to consider, then I'll be happy to present it to them."

It almost doesn't matter what number gets thrown out after such a request—any number response shows the first step in detaching from the name. Once that happens, the negotiation can begin.

Over a couple months of correspondence, we ended up with a price Frida Baby and the domain owner were both happy with. In the process, I educated them both on the safety and security of the transaction so that everyone could walk away with what they wanted. The seller dictated some terms—such as a request to have emails forwarded for sixty days, which was an easy ask for my client to agree to.

When people come to the negotiation table, they want to feel like they're winning. In the end, everyone left the table feeling like they had won. The seller got more money than she'd ever been offered from years of lowball offers—and the buyer knew how valuable the domain name was for their long-term growth. It ended up being on the shorter side of sales cycles with the transaction being finalized a few months after the company had first reached out to me.

I have little doubt that the shift from FridaBaby.com to Frida.com has been a net positive for the company. Around the same time they acquired the premium domain name, they launched a new offering—Frida Mom—and the company boasts an impressive 70 percent market share in their main category, according to their LinkedIn overview.[51]

Like I mentioned in the last chapter, it's nearly impossible to find an original, available, and optimal one-word .COM. As your company grows, acquiring the premium domain name becomes not only more urgent, but also necessary to promote long-term growth.

Most of the time, acquiring an existing domain name is a strategic transaction. That is, it's not the same as an investor who has purchased domain names because they appreciate in value just like stocks and real estate. The transaction has a strategic business purpose—such as driving more traffic like in the Honeymoons.com story from Chapter 10 or asserting your brand like with Frida Baby.

So we're going to shift our focus here to look specifically at how you go about acquiring an existing domain name, especially when it's in active use like in the Frida story. How do you begin the process of winning your ideal domain name?

NAME YOUR PRICE

The unfortunate but unavoidable truth is you have to start with price. The most important question you have to weigh is "What's your budget?" So think about it: What is the name truly worth to you?

If you start too low, then the seller won't see you as a serious contender and you may have lost your chance to start a dialogue. It's like raising the paddle at an auction—you better know how high you're willing to go.

Time also plays a factor here. While the Frida transaction only took a few months, a big part of that was because the buyer was highly motivated and willing to pay what the seller asked for. You can try to get the lowest price possible or you can try to get it quickly—but you can't do both.

DOMAIN NAME AUCTIONS & NEWSLETTERS

Speaking of auctions, you might recall that in my early days in the industry, my business partner and I held domain name auctions at different conferences around the world. These auctions are still around and a viable option. In fact, sometimes they are the *only* option when a seller has decided they want to invite a bidding war.

When I helped my client obtain Lawn.com, it was done through an auction. The previous owner of the registration wanted to fetch top dollar, knowing how valuable of a domain name they had on their hands.

To this day, I still help clients looking for names going up for auction, which is another way a broker can assist.

A few auctions to look into:

- Afternic (owned by GoDaddy)
- Brannans
- Dan (owned by GoDaddy)
- Efty (designed with investors in mind)
- Flippa
- GoDaddy Auction
- Namecheap
- ROTD
- Sedo

Likewise, you can find newsletters within the domain name industry where you can scout out names for sale. Oftentimes, these are owners who are eager to liquidate so it can be a quicker process. At Brannan's, we actually have our own newsletter we send out to top domainers and domain name investors all across the world. If domain name investing is of interest to you, it's a good place to start.

So if you've already set a budget to what you want to spend on a domain name but you're undecided, newsletters and auctions can be a great option to find your brand.

DROPCATCH SERVICES

Dropcatching sounds like some kind of slang for an error being made in baseball, but in short, it's the practice of buying a domain name when the registrant fails to renew it—whether on purpose or not.

When a domain name "drops," it means that it's becoming available again for registration. Whole businesses have been set up to watch for these drops so that potential buyers can snap them up when they drop.

These are particularly good to know about if you're interested in becoming an investor and flipping names. Essentially, you register on the sites, look through the names that are at risk for dropping and then tell them which names you're interested in. Some services even allow you to set up alerts so you can stay on top of names if they become available.

There's always a short grace period for owners to catch a dropped name before someone else can snap it up, but once that grace period is over, it's fair game. So these automated services allow you to buy the name within milliseconds of it becoming available, even though you might be at work, running an errand, or walking the dog when it happens.

Some services you might want to look into for dropcatching include the following:

- DropCatch
- GoDaddy
- HexoNet
- NameJet
- SnapNames

A best practice is to register whichever name you're interested in across all dropcatching services. You never know how many other investors out there are interested in the same name, so you want to give yourself the best chance of catching it.

FIND THE OWNER

Way back in Chapter 3, I mentioned how being a domain broker can sometimes feel like being a private investigator. While you can certainly look at WHOIS databases to track down the owner of the domain name you want, these days so much of the information is privacy-protected. It's going to take more than a search query, especially for a more premium name.

You'll need to perform immense due diligence to ensure you don't end up communicating with a scam artist who has hacked the email of the true owner. Given the international market of the domain name industry, you need to be sure you know who the owner is and where they are located.

FIND OUT WHO BUYS DOMAIN NAMES

If you discover the owner of the domain registration isn't an individual but a corporate entity, then you'll have some extra steps to take. You'll need to track down whoever it is at the company who is responsible for domain name acquisition and management because they will likely also be the person involved in any discussions about selling. At the very least, they will know who you need to connect with.

Depending on how large the corporate entity is, you can expect it to be more of a group discussion. While they may have an executive in charge of Intellectual Property or Trademark, the decision to sell a domain name will often land on the agenda for a C-Suite or board meeting. And probably not just one meeting.

But knowing who your primary contact is will determine what kind of discussion you need to start with. A marketing department head will view your offer differently from someone in IT or someone on the legal team. Either way, when dealing with a large corporation, you need to buckle up and prepare for a longer transaction period—anywhere from three months to a few years.

Don't let that timeframe discourage you if it's really your top choice domain name. The only way to find out the real timeframe is to engage the company that owns the domain name or engage the services of a broker so they can engage the domain owner on your behalf. Generally within one to three months, you'll know what the situation is on any given domain name.

And on that note, recognize that given the security and brand issues a corporation has to account for with their IP and intangible assets, there are more stakeholders who can say "No" than in a typical buying arrangement. At any moment, someone from the C-Suite, marketing/branding, legal, or even IT could veto the conversation and shut down the opportunity for a sale even when they initially were open to selling.

If at any point, the response back to you is "I'm not sure," then you can go ahead and interpret it as a "No" to moving forward. You have to understand the issue from their side: If they still have active trademarks, systems, and data attached to the domain name, then there may not be any dollar amount worth the sale for them.

And even if you are able to offer them an interesting price which makes all the work of untangling systems worth it, you can still expect it to be quite some time before the registration is transferred to you. So you have to ask yourself, "Is this name worth it to me? Can my brand wait multiple years to upgrade?"

WHEN THE NAME IS "NOT FOR SALE"

In the above corporate example, the domain name in question may not be publicly "for sale," but obviously, this is because the company still has some passive use for it. But what if a name is "not for sale" and *not* being used at all?

Don't be surprised when the name you want is unavailable but also not being actively used. There's a big difference between a name being unavailable because an investor has it parked until they get the price they want and someone who has no plans to sell the name whatsoever.

But just because it's "not for sale" doesn't mean it can't be bought. Like in the opening Frida story, you will just need help. We'll circle back to this more in the next chapter, but the "Not For Sale" sign is often actually a good indicator that you need a domain name broker in your corner.

UNDERSTANDING & NEGOTIATING WITH A DOMAIN OWNER

Like in the Frida story, sometimes the owner of a domain name isn't interested in money. So it doesn't matter what number you throw out, they won't be convinced. In such cases, it requires a deeper understanding of human psychology.

They may not want money—but they might want to be able to put their grandchildren through college, or take that once-in-a-lifetime trip, or start up a charitable foundation that will outlive them. Only once you've identified what a domain owner truly wants can you even begin to negotiate.

As a reminder, it's a bad move at this point to try a "strong arm" approach to wrest away the domain name. If you think you can go get a trademark and force someone to give you the domain name, think again. Your shiny new trademark won't undo the fact they have owned the name for twenty-plus years. So don't be surprised when they jack up the price further just to teach you a lesson after they kick your ass in a WIPO or in US Federal court.

Strong negotiating skills come with time. If the seller is even a moderately skilled negotiator and they hear the urgency in your voice, you can bet the price will go up. You've got to be very careful with the language you use, walking a delicate balance between urgency and interest. Oh yeah—all while building trust along the way. Many sellers aren't going to sell their domain name to someone they don't like.

Oftentimes, this is where having a middleman comes in handy—like a broker. My job demands I be more emotionally unattached from the outcome while still working to get my clients the best possible deal—and gaining trust with the seller. When there are attorneys involved on both sides (and with a premium name, there will be), then taking care with your language becomes even more important.

DOMAIN AGREEMENTS, ESCROW & TRANSFER

Whether it's a company selling to a company, an individual selling to a company, or a company selling to an individual, you'll need a domain agreement before anything can happen. It's in the interest of both parties to ensure everything is squared away and on the up and up.

A twenty page agreement doesn't raise my pulse and after so many years of working with attorneys on transactions, I can even redline and comment any clauses which cause me concern so I can advise clients.

The same is true if you're working for a company looking to acquire a new domain name. I've done many corporate transactions, so I can recognize what clauses need to be in there to protect the company's interests. In either event, I have a standard agreement to help buyers and sellers through the process.

As far as the purchase process, it's not so different from the escrow process in a real estate transaction—the agent will make sure the client gets the home, that the bank gets the collateral documents, and that the seller gets the money. In fact, Escrow.com is the service used for domain name transactions because of how secure it is. (You can read more about this in Section IV, Chapters 17, 18 and 19.)

Once upon a time, domain name transfers were done on paper—but now they can all be done digitally. It's a far simpler process than it used to be.

At GoDaddy, a transfer from one company's account to another company's account is called an "Account Change" and it literally only takes seconds for the transfer to happen. In my experience, with GoDaddy you've got the best security for the process because they have teams of professionals who can help. If somehow a domain name registration is stolen by a cybercriminal, I've found them to be the most responsive to help recover it.

Just like with acquiring a new name, you want to make sure the email on file for the registration is never assigned to a single person. Don't have Bob@CompanyName be the registrant. One day Bob will retire, get fired, leave, or die. And if no one knows that the domain was assigned to Bob's email, and it's no longer being monitored, then the registration could lapse and get snapped up by an investor or another company—or it could become vulnerable to a security breach.

Once that's all done, the name is yours—along with the benefits it will bring!

CONCLUSION

You've probably heard the Chinese proverb, "The best time to plant a tree was thirty years ago, the second best time is now." You could say the same is true for domain names as premium names continue to become more scarce, and therefore, more valuable.

Case in point—Gold.com. As I'm writing this, Gold.com has just changed hands again. A few years back, Kay Jewelers spent around $3 million to acquire it, and now they've unloaded it to someone else in the bullion business, for $8.5 million! And Rocket.com just sold for $14 million (2024).

While you shouldn't rush into buying a domain name—especially a premium one—without doing your homework, you also should drag your feet. Follow the steps covered in the last two chapters and you'll be able to keep yourself moving forward at a healthy pace.

You've probably noticed it's nearly impossible to describe this process without also describing the role a broker plays, especially when you're dealing with a premium name. But before you go out into the wide world to find your domain name, you'll need to know when it's right to hire a domain broker to come alongside and help make the process more seamless and secure.

CHAPTER 12

WHEN TO HIRE A DOMAIN BROKER

UCH OF WHAT is discussed in this chapter was also covered in Chapter 3 in the section about brokers. However, if you came straight to this section of the book because you're looking at buying a domain name, the most pertinent information is still covered here, along with some additional information specific to acquiring a domain name.

But the main point of this chapter is not so much *what* we do as brokers or *why* we do it. It's about *when*—the right timing to enlist the services of a domain broker.

In short, you could hire a domain broker at any time you're considering buying a domain name. But it would be wrong to assume you always need a broker. So let's take a closer look at the *when*.

WHEN YOU'RE ASSESSING A NAME

Business owners should consult at least four professionals when starting an endeavor—two cost money and the other two are free.

The two who cost money are an attorney and an accountant. You want to pick professionals who are going to take you to the next level. In the case of an attorney, you want someone who asks solid "what if" questions to keep you from standing on a figurative landmine—such as the trademark and IP issues we've already covered.

With an accountant, I always advise going with someone local to you. As much as can be done digitally these days, it's still best practice to pull out financial statements in person rather than over a screen. Just my two cents.

The first free professional is a banker. Sometimes in business, you need to be able to get a signature on a loan quickly—so it's good to have a banker who knows you, knows what you do, and will help you get the money you need fast. Money is the most expensive purchase you'll ever make, so have a good banker. This could come in very handy if you end up needing to finance a great domain name.

And finally, there's the insurance agent. You should always be able to reach out to someone familiar with your business that you can call with insurance questions.

If I had to pick a fifth professional, I'd suggest a domain broker. While our actual services aren't free, per se, the initial consultation is. If you've ever sat down with a real estate agent, then you know one of the first questions they ask is, "What are you looking for?" And then they'll take notes as you tell them exactly what type of property you want. From there, they can make recommendations on specific neighborhoods to look at or properties they already know about which match your description.

Likewise, I'm always happy to advise people in search of a domain name for their brand. It's not unusual for me to meet people who believe the myths that they can be successful with a multi-word SLD (e.g., GetMyService), a keyword-based SLD (e.g.,BestPlumberAtlanta), or an alternate TLD like .BIZ or .TEL.

This would be similar to the homebuyer who is only looking at a price on a house but not considering that it's located in a neighborhood with the highest crime rate for the entire city. My first job is to put their interests first and coach them with much of the same information presented throughout this book concerning what makes a great domain name—and what doesn't.

Always talk to the free professionals first—the bankers and domain name brokers. Shop around a couple of banks, credit unions, and figure out who you trust and who can grow with your needs.

I've taken on free consultations with all kinds of people. I don't see it as a waste of my time because I'm always eager to hear what people are doing, especially when they are thinking ahead long-term with their business strategy.

WHEN YOU'RE DEALING WITH 5 FIGURES (AND UP)

Pricing plays a major factor in when to hire a domain broker. If the domain name you're looking at is under $10K, it's probably not the right fit for a broker. If it's over $10K, then it's time to talk because it means the transaction will require more than a couple clicks of a button.

Like many founders discover, pricing can be a roadblock. But if they are serious about growth, then they are going to put everything they have into getting that domain name. I've consistently seen how the scrappy entrepreneurs who finance their domain names are the least likely to default on their payments. They'll sell off just about every other asset before they will let go of their premium domain name!

The higher the dollar sign attached to the name, the more complex the deal can become. The agreements will be longer, the negotiations more delicate, and you can bet there will be attorneys involved. If you wouldn't try to purchase a house or building without the help of a realtor, chances are you shouldn't risk buying a $10K+ domain name on your own either.

WHEN YOU WANT TO AVOID MISTAKES

It's not difficult to make mistakes with domain name acquisitions. Maybe you choose a name that is trademarked by someone else and find yourself in trademark court, shelling out cash on legal fees. Maybe you find yourself in federal court because the domain name you bought was owned by a business and the employee who sold it to you didn't have the authority to do so. Maybe the person you've been dealing with turns out to be a cybercriminal—and they've run off with your money and you don't have the domain you thought you had secured.

If a domain broker has been in the industry for any substantial time— ten or more years—they'll know what to watch out for. They'll save you from making these mistakes—and more.

Deals can get especially dicey when they become international transactions—which happens frequently in our industry. Not only do you have to navigate language and cultural nuances in the negotiation but also international law. A broker's job is to navigate around the various snares so you get the outcome you're looking for.

In short, while it's good to learn from your mistakes, it's even better to avoid the mistakes altogether. Especially when those mistakes could cost you everything you have.

WHEN YOU NEED A SKILLED NEGOTIATOR

Part of the fun with domain name transactions is the negotiation. There are never two that are completely alike. One day I can be negotiating with a CFO at a large, publicly-traded company—and the next, it could be a business-savvy widow who discovers a high-value domain name among the estate's assets. And then the very next day, I might be playing middleman between a stalwart Chinese executive and a Stanford dropout-turned-founder.

After twenty-plus years and thousands of transactions, I've seen almost everything. You can't survive long in this industry if you don't know how to negotiate.

Negotiation is both an art and science. It requires great skill in reading the room, understanding human psychology, while also exercising broad knowledge in the deal itself. It's a whole different ball game than talking a car salesman and their sales manager down ten thousand bucks.

When it comes to domain names, there's more to negotiate about than simply the price. Details of how the transfer will occur, how the domain name is going to be used, and security all come into play. These are issues that not everyone is going to know how to handle if you've never done it before. They are also the issues which will absolutely kill the deal if you don't handle them well—even if you're offering a great price.

CONCLUSION

You might recall from Chapter 3 that there are no industry-wide rules for how domain brokers work. The systems and standards we follow are largely the result of years of trial and error and figuring out what works. Like in real estate, we mostly set our own fees for transactions, but 15 percent of the final sales price tends to be the go-to standard.

You may find some "discount brokers" who only charge 10 percent on a deal, but either they are newer brokers who can only handle certain, easier transactions, or you simply won't be receiving the same level of service as a more experienced broker. Sometimes this might only become obvious during the negotiation phase when it might be too late to back out.

More often than not, you get what you pay for—so you're better off getting a broker who is comfortable and confident enough to speak to anyone in the C-Suite and bring them into the negotiation. Especially once you're looking at a transaction upwards of $50K, or an international deal, it's not the time to go cut-rate.

There's still one more *when* for hiring a broker, though it's related to the negotiation itself—and that's when you need help *financing* a domain name. We'll take a closer look at that process in the next chapter.

CHAPTER 13

DOMAIN NAME FINANCING

I**T'S NOT UNCOMMON** for founders and entrepreneurs to find themselves in a painful position: They know what domain name they need. The owner is willing to talk. But the price far exceeds what they have available in their pockets. And as you now know for yourself, they are aware that the name is only going to go up in value—or, that it could get bought by someone else before they can raise the capital. What would you do?

Turns out the solution is an incredibly common one—you finance the premium domain name.

Not everyone needs to finance the domain name of their dreams, but it's certainly an option I've helped founders and entrepreneurs with over the years—even with domain names with seven-figure valuations. And as I've mentioned before, the finance deals on premium names very rarely default when compared to the finance deals under $10K.

While this is a shorter chapter, it's still an important topic you should know about. It might very well mean the domain name you want—the one that feels out of reach—may actually be more feasible than you thought.

It should be mentioned first, however, that as a broker, I do not offer any kind of financing of domain names myself. That's beyond the scope of the broker-client relationship. However, when I'm working with a client who is interested in financing the purchase, I can lend them my expertise to find the best possible deal for their situation.

So with that out of the way—what kind of finance options are available for domain names?

OWNER-FINANCED

You might recall from the LasVegas.com story that the domain name was purchased for $90 million—but over a thirty year term. While the exact details of this arrangement are not public, I'd venture a guess this is a case where they are financing the purchase from the previous owner.

If you're buying a domain name from a corporation or a high net-worth individual, these deals can be particularly attractive for the seller. After all, they don't have much to lose. They get guaranteed income in the form of a monthly payment—and if the loan defaults, the domain name reverts back to them, and they get to keep all of the payments that have been made—and then they can also offer it up to someone else.

Once you've got someone to the table, it's always worth asking if they are open to the idea. Not everyone will be—some sellers would rather have the deal done, money in their pocket, and not have to think about it anymore.

DOMAIN CAPITAL

Domain Capital, doing business at DomainCapital.com, helps companies buy domain names by financing the purchase. That's their business model. They've been around since 2006 and they're leaders in domain financing. If financing will be needed, it makes sense to reach out to them.

INSTITUTION-FINANCED

If the owner is not willing to finance, then buyers can always choose to go a more traditional route and take out a loan with a bank or credit union. You might recall in the last chapter, we talked about the importance of having a banker on your team. This is one of the times when a close relationship with a banker could come in handy.

If they know your business and understand the investment aspect of a premium domain name, then it de-risks the loan for the bank compared to someone who walks in off the street and says they need $500K for their business.

After all, no one wants to lose their job over a bad loan. But you can make a stronger business case for the loan when your banker has seen your P&L statements and has a more intimate knowledge of how a premium domain name will boost your market share.

INVESTOR-FINANCED

Let's say you're still in the fundraising stage of your startup but it becomes prudent to upgrade to a premium domain name. In the same way you would do a fundraising round to support development of new products or distribution, you could go to investors and do a round specifically for the premium domain name.

Like with a bank, you'll need to be able to prove why the purchase is good for the business. But if you have a good relationship with investors who are already seeing their money put to good use, then it could be low-hanging fruit to acquire that premium domain name which will boost traffic, boost sales, and therefore, boost the return for the investors.

CONCLUSION

Financing a domain name is a huge decision which shouldn't be taken lightly. However, there are a couple of benefits which are worth considering:

1. **Financing forces you to think long-term.** When you're on the hook for a finance deal that stretches over the course of one to four years, it tends to light a fire under you. It gives you more skin in the game, another reason to get up every morning and do everything in your power to be successful.

2. **Financing lets you have and use the premium domain name now.** Remember, it will never be cheaper than it is today. So you get the market benefit of having the premium .COM address—the increased web traffic, increased customer trust, and increased revenue. Plus, you get the benefit of the domain name itself gaining value as an asset for the company. If you ever decide to sell the company, the domain name itself will remain a line item with its own value attached to it.

3. **Owning a premium domain name opens doors.** Remember, National MRI Scan had only raised a pre-seed round when they bought Scan.com with owner financing for three years. Since that purchase, they've raised $65 million (as of October, 2024).

As with any financial decision, you should talk with your accountant about your options before entering any kind of finance agreement. But once you're ready to move ahead, an experienced broker will be able to help you integrate the finance details into the deal to ensure a smooth process for both sides.

CHAPTER 14

HOW TO HANDLE CYBERSQUATTERS

T HE PROBLEM WITH any high-value asset is that they tend to attract the attention of criminals. You have probably heard of cases where cybercriminals hacked into a system and stole data from an organization, holding it ransom. In some cases, they hold an entire website for ransom unless the owners cough up whatever they are asking for.

We've spoken extensively already about doing your own due diligence to make sure you're not infringing on someone else's IP or trademark, but what do you do when you find someone else using your name—or even, a variation on your name in a questionable way?

WHAT IS CYBERSQUATTING?

Cybersquatting is the act of someone purposefully registering a domain name which is very similar to a known trademark or piece of IP. Often, the cybersquatters are not actually using the name for any purpose other than to "squat" on it. They may simply want to prevent the true brand from registering it in the hope the brand will later buy it off of them, or they may even decide to set it up with ads so that they can generate revenue from the people who end up there because of the name.

In the early days of the internet, well-known brands were targeted—especially if they didn't own their exact match .COM yet. Cybersquatters would buy up the domains and wait for the brands to realize what had happened.

One of the earliest big cases to actually go to court involved a group of cybersquatters who targeted Burger King in the UK. In 1998, cyber-squatters bought the name BurgerKing.co.uk before the fast food chain thought to acquire the name for themselves. Not that Burger King should be faulted for this—not many people were thinking about domain names in 1998.

But it became a sticky issue when they approached Burger King about buying it from them for the sum of £25K (about $40K in 1998 dollars). Obviously, Burger King felt like their trademark was being willfully infringed upon, so they took it to court.[52]

Some cybersquatters are even more nefarious, using domain names to scam people. While in the process of writing this book and learning about publishing, I discovered a common scam involving companies who call themselves some variation of "Amazon Publishing" in order to trick aspiring authors into using their services.

One of these scams even had fake reviews which had been obviously generated with AI, including from authors like James Joyce and Gabriel Garcia Marquez—who are both deceased and therefore unable to write such a review. Unfortunately, these red flags can be easily missed if you don't know to look for them. Last I checked, Amazon was taking legal action against these bad actors since it impacts their brand reputation.

Sometimes the cybersquatting is less obvious, such as an intentional misspelling or variation on the name. For instance, instead of Walmart. com, a cybersquatter might try to use something like Wal-MartStors. com. Or you might recall from Chapter 6, the lawsuits won by Verizon against a cybersquatter who had registered over 600 names related to their trademarks.

LEGAL ACTIONS TO TAKE

What makes cybersquatting difficult, of course, is that not everyone has the resources or an army of expensive attorneys behind them like Burger King, Amazon, or Verizon do. For smaller businesses, though, there are still some resources to consider.

RESEARCH

First, you need to start with some research to investigate if the incident in question actually is a case of cybersquatting. Start with visiting the questionable domain and see if there is a website set up or not. It may be that they simply have a similar name but no intentional infringement is happening. In fact, if their offerings are nothing like your own, then it's probably no more than a case of similar names, like with the Graco case mentioned in Chapter 9.

Larger, richer companies have the resources to be more litigious if they want to be—but it might be a waste of your time, especially if your name is common in English. For instance, no one should be surprised that there is more than one "Smith's Bakery," or "Deluxe Dry Cleaners."

CEASE & DESIST LETTER

But let's say your research shows someone may actually be trying to infringe on your brand and take traffic away from you or cause confusion. Meet with your attorney since they are one of the professionals you should have on your team—and have them draft a cease and desist letter.

In some cases, this is enough to stop someone. They may drop the name of their own accord and disappear, moving on to infringe on someone else's trademark.

ACPA SUIT

If your business is in the United States, one option is to sue the cybersquatter in accordance with the Anticybersquatting Consumer Protection Act, which was passed in 1999 once the first cases of cybersquatting started to reach courts.

To have a case, you'll need to be able to prove the cybersquatter is infringing on your trademark with "a bad-faith intent to profit from the trademark," as well as showing proof you owned the trademark before the offending domain name was registered."

The difficulty with these lawsuits is that the defendant could be able to prove they had a good reason to register the domain name in a way that doesn't violate your trademark. If they do, then they get to keep the name and you're out a bunch of money for legal fees.

Also, a bad actor could choose to disappear and not show up to court—especially if they are already based overseas. The good news is there is also legal action you can take on an international level.

ICANN PROCEDURE

Also in 1999, ICANN created the Uniform Domain Name Dispute Resolution Policy (UDRP or UDNRP). However, it should be noted this is not for litigation purposes, but for arbitration between two parties over a name.

Still, if the complainant can prove infringement, then the offending domain name could be canceled or transferred over to the complainant. However, you should be aware that the policy does not permit for any financial remuneration like the ACPA does.[53]

CONCLUSION

Ultimately, you have to decide what action is worth your time and money. Some people even decide it's worth it to just pay off the cybersquatters and make them relinquish the domain name. I personally never advise doing this because doing so will likely invite the same cybersquatter—or their buddies—to do the same with a new domain name.

Yet this is one more consideration to make when you're assembling your ideas for brand names. If some similar spellings or variations of your names can be bought cheaply, it might be worth the investment if for no other reason than preventing cybersquatters from taking those names later on as you grow and attract more attention.

You can't control what others do—but you can control what you do. So the best move you can make is to protect your IP by getting your trademark. After all, your domain name might end up being your most valuable asset, so you better protect it.

SECTION IV

SELLING A PREMIUM DOMAIN NAME

CHAPTER 15

DO YOU HAVE A PREMIUM DOMAIN NAME?

IN 2009, I was approached by a domain name owner. He had heard of Brannans and our reputation for selling premium, one-word, .COMs. As for the domain name he was looking to sell?

Christian.com.

As you can imagine, such a name has mass appeal. For one thing, it's a proper name. But more importantly, it's a name that holds massive meaning for a large number of people around the world.

One aspect of domains we haven't discussed yet is the role we brokers play in the selling process. We're not just there to facilitate the actual sale—but also to identify all the potential buyers. It's part of our job to make sure we get everyone to the table who needs to be there.

Long before the auction, we started marketing the name's availability, alerting everyone we could think of who might be interested—large religious institutions like megachurches and seminaries—anyone you could consider the "Who's Who" of Christianity in the English-speaking world. By doing so, we uncovered all the prospective buyers, getting them interested in the auction.

Some of these groups were not only interested in the name itself but also had an interest in protecting the name and making sure it wouldn't fall into the hands of a bad actor. For instance, they wouldn't want a hate group like the infamous Westboro Baptist Church to acquire the name and misuse it.

On the day of the auction, everyone was happy with the final result— the buyer, the seller, and myself. What's interesting about the buyer is that he was actually an investor who ended up selling again later on. As I was writing this chapter, I discovered the name is up for grabs yet again.

Just goes to show that once a name is premium, it often remains premium—and it's always a domain someone else would want.

But most importantly, when you're dealing with a high-value, premium domain name, you have to establish a ton of trust. The seller came to me because of my reputation in the industry, yes, but it was the transparency in the process that kept him around all the way through auction.

Likewise, if you believe you have a premium domain name on your hands, you need to take great care who you trust with the sale. These can be complicated and complex deals where you're dealing with not only large sums of money, but international law, IP and trademark issues, and more.

THE PREMIUM TEST

Before you go slapping a price on a name and trying to sell it, you first need to figure out whether you've actually got a premium domain name on your hands. Fifty to a hundred times a week, we get calls and emails about domain names that owners think could be premium.

Unfortunately, most of these will fail the test of being an actual premium name. And almost always, the call starts off the same: "I have 200 domain names that I think have value . . ."

Rather than let people suffer in the delusion, I've always taken the transparency route to tell people the names aren't worth what they think they are. In fact, I've even told some people, "That name's not even worth the renewal fee—you'd be better off to let the registration drop."

As long as I've been doing this job, I can typically scan a list of a hundred names and spot any that have real potential. Usually, it follows more of a process of elimination, so to help you do the same, here's exactly what I do:

- Automatically exclude anything that's not a .COM.
- Exclude any SLD that has three or more words. For instance, "BuyACar," or "RealEstateAgentNewYork."
- Exclude anything that's not in the dictionary. Typically, any kind of gibberish, such as "hs84d.COM," is worthless.

Once those have all been rooted out, you're left with a much easier list to gauge potential. That's when I go back to the staples we've covered before:

- One-word SLD attached to a .COM
- Easy to spell/correctly spelled
- Registered before 2000

If it passes those tests, you might have something great on your hands!

The problem with many of the requests I see is that people want to convince themselves they have a fantastic domain name on their hands. They will write a 1,500-word email explaining why it's valuable. But what I've found to be true is that the premium domains speak for themselves—they don't need any justifying.

Unfortunately, this sometimes means someone finds out they overpaid for the name. Some shyster convinced them to buy the name as an investment and they ended up paying ten times what it's actually worth. Not too long ago, I helped someone in such a situation who had bought a name in the six-figure range but when he needed to liquidate, he found out the name was only worth in the five-figure range. It was a terrible situation.

Sometimes people like to object with the test of "correctly spelled." They'll point at "Google" and "Verizon" as examples of misspelled and made-up words with premium value. But these are the exceptions to the rule. Their domain names have great value because the companies themselves are high-value organizations.

The truth is that of the over 367 million registered domain names, most of them are not premium. There are probably only about twenty to thirty thousand domain names which can pass "The Premium Test."

As a best practice, if you're reaching out to a broker about a name you have and you think it might have some premium potential, just write a short intro email. Two short sentences are plenty. Honestly, I take those *far* more seriously than the long emails.

Another red flag I look for is the person who contacts me is trying to sell a name related to a trademarked brand or term. For instance, if someone came to me saying, "I own the domain name TVApple.com and I want to sell it to Apple."

Usually, this is a sign of someone who doesn't understand IP and trademark law. At best, they will embarrass themselves when no one takes the offer seriously. At worst, they could end up in court for violating Apple's trademark on AppleTV by essentially holding the domain name "for ransom." And if Apple takes them to court, they will win and *each* infringing domain name will cost the registrant $50,000.

As a best practice, when you are reaching out to a broker about a name you want to sell, it's best if you know there will be more than one potential buyer interested. A broker worth their salt wants to get as many buyers to the table as possible. It can take months—even years—to sell a premium name, so that's a lot of time and work to ask from someone if you only have one potential buyer in mind. Plus, it's only in *your* best interest to have multiple buyers who will help drive the sale price up.

EMOTIONAL ATTACHMENT

One of Dale Carnegie's most famous quotes is all about the emotional connection we have to our own name: "A person's name is to that person the sweetest and most important sound in any language."[54] It was true when he wrote those words in 1936 and it's still true now.

As mentioned back in Section III, the largest hurdle you may have to selling your premium domain name is the emotional attachment you have with the name. Perhaps it's a family name, or the name of a business you started even if it's no longer active. The idea of selling something so personal may feel like selling a piece of yourself.

You might be surprised just how often this exact situation comes up. A few years ago, I was approached by a steak company who was very interested in the name "Wilders." It was the brand name they had settled on for their company—and they wanted to make sure their brand was best positioned by having the exact .COM match.

When I went into investigation mode, I discovered that the owners of Wilders.com also had the last name of "Wilder." They had registered it years before but had never actually used it, unlike the Frida.com story

I shared where the domain was being used for email. But once we were able to help the owner emotionally detach from the name, they realized they were never going to use it—but could definitely use the money from the sale to do some good.

If you find yourself in this position, try to think about what you could do with the proceeds from a sale. Would selling the domain name pay for your children's or grandchildren's college tuition? Could it fund a foundation devoted to a cause you care about? Could it ensure that your loved ones are taken care of after you're gone? That last point may be a little too close to home but consider this: You may know what your domain name is worth but your heirs may not believe you even when you've told them so for decades.

Remember, at the end of the day, it's not just about the money but what it can do for you and your family.

Over the years, we've been able to help many domain owners transform their domain name into wealth—often in the six figures and even seven figure ranges. Obviously, the seven figure range is more difficult to hit, but when the domain name is really good, I've helped clients do exactly that!

CORPORATE ATTACHMENT

Maybe you found yourself in this section of the book because you work for a corporation and you've been given the exciting assignment of figuring out what to do with your company's digital assets. Perhaps you just went through a merger—or maybe the company is doing some structural "house cleaning" and wants to find anything non-essential to liquidate to help boost the next quarterly report.

When mergers and acquisitions happen, it's inevitable for some domain names to be thrown into the mix of acquired assets. As mentioned in Section III, corporations take the longest to decide on selling a domain name—and for good reason. Here are a few questions you should be considering if you find yourself looking at a slate of corporate-owned digital assets:

DO WE HAVE THE ACCESS WE NEED TO MAINTAIN ASSET OWNERSHIP?

For instance, if the domain name you acquired has a Registrant and Admin contact of Bob@AcquiredCompany.com, then first, who is Bob? Second, is Bob still part of this new company? Should he even have access to the registrar account in question, which for all intents and purposes, gives him the ability to transfer the domain name if he decides to?

Last point here, leaving Bob@AcquiredCompany.com as the email can also open you up to all kinds of security risks, including a bad actor infiltrating Bob's old email and taking ownership of the name for themselves.If you don't know what Bob's password protocols were, then his password to the account might end up on the dark web one day.

Regardless of the answer to the above questions, you should change Registrant information for all corporate domain names to one Registrar (I like GoDaddy) and using a generic email like Domains@CompanyName.com. Keep in mind that making any changes will effectively lock a domain name against registrar transfer for sixty days. Still, as a housekeeping item, it's a good practice to use a role-based email for your company's domain names.

If you're not able to maintain ownership by being able to access the corresponding registration email, logging in, and renewing the domain name, then you run two risks. First, you risk losing the domain name because you fail to receive the notification that the registration is about to expire. Second, this will present quite a hurdle to selling the domain should you ever choose to do so.

DO WE HAVE SYSTEMS AND DATA ATTACHED TO THE ASSET?

If the domain name was also being used as part of a storage server or email server, then there could still be some sensitive proprietary information attached to it—including confidential information about employees, intellectual property, and even company records.

If you're not sure, then it's time to pull in the CIO (Chief Information

Officer) and/or CISO (Chief Information Security Officer) to take a look at everything. You should always get IT to check for any potential vulnerabilities before you entertain the idea of selling it.

HAVE WE PERFORMED DUE DILIGENCE?

We've talked about this multiple times now but it truly cannot be overstated. Before selling any digital asset, you must do your due diligence. It's the perfect time to bring in both a broker and a lawyer who specifically has domain name experience. The problem with some companies is they try to only utilize their own legal team, not realizing how different domain name transactions can be.

Before you sell, you need to be able to verify who you are selling to and where they are located so that you're not breaking any federal or international laws. You should also have crystal clear language around how the domain name is going to be used so it doesn't create a problem for your company in the future.

For example, it's normal for a corporate seller to insert a No-Compete clause dictating that the buyer cannot be in direct competition with the seller. Or in the event of a seller-financed transaction, they want to ensure the registration reverts back to them if the buyer defaults on payments (more on this in Chapter 18).

But once you have answered all these questions, dotted your I's and crossed your T's, then you can proceed forward with selling your premium domain name.

VALUATION TOOLS

We talked in the last section about exercising caution with valuation tools from a buyer perspective, but what if you're looking to sell a domain name? Is the advice any different here?

For the most part, it's the same. The algorithm-based valuation tools like Estibot are more or less useless. Simply put, none of these tools can accurately predict the final sale price because domain names are illiquid assets and the domain name industry is a bit like the Wild West. I've seen tools that both overvalued and under-valued domain names. And just like that sticker price they put on the car at the dealership, once you see the number, it's difficult to un-see it.

So if you've already used one of the valuation tools out there, take the number it spat out with a hefty serving of salt and skepticism. I've sometimes received emails from individuals claiming a certain number because of what a valuation tool told them—and yet literally no one has ever reached out to make an offer to them. But it's like trying to sell a car with no engine—it's not going very far no matter what the sticker says!

You would be better off consulting with an industry insider—such as myself—to gain more clarity. But even I would only be giving you an educated guess based on experience. The true value of your domain name comes down to two factors:

1.   What you're willing to let it go for.
2.   What someone is willing to pay for it.

Since the domain name industry is largely unregulated, it truly is that simple. There are no minimums which must be met—nor maximums imposed. But a quick scan of the top-selling domain names of all time can give you an idea of the upper limits. On our <u>website</u>,[55] we actually have a page devoted to the top 150 domain name valuations and even #150 tops seven figures.

If you're a high-net worth individual, then the amount you're willing to let it go for will likely be much higher compared to someone who needs to liquidate quickly. And even if you have a one-word, easy-to-spell .COM you've had since 1995, pricing it at $2 million won't mean much if no one is willing to pay for it.

You can go back to Chapter 5 to read more about the valuation tiers and in Chapter 16, we'll get into how a broker helps with valuation since it can also overlap with the negotiation process. It's natural you should want to get more than you hoped—but accomplishing this often means the buyer needs to feel like they're getting a steal.

FILTERING PROSPECTS

When it comes to filtering prospects, the best action you can take is to create a folder in a tool like Dropbox or Google Drive and save any email inquiries you have received about your domain name over the years. The most interesting—and valuable—domain names will receive hundreds of offers for at least a decade. This category includes your short, three-letter domain names and .COMs. Even if you're not ready to sell quite yet, create the folder and start adding any and all inquiry emails to it.

I do exactly the same for the domain names I hold onto as investments. It can be a great cue for not only valuation but also for honing in on the ideal type of buyer I should be marketing the name to.

Once someone engages our services, the very next action we take is to send an email asking them to forward us every email they've ever received about their domain name.

This often surprises people and they will say, "Are you sure? I've received hundreds."

Our response is always, "Yes, we're a hundred percent serious. Send them all!"

A couple of reasons for this:

For one, because I need to see what kind of offers have already been made. Even if there are some obvious lowball offers, it's helpful to figure out where the floor is for a future auction.

But the main reason is that I've found at least half of these inquiries will be from people who I know in the business. Often, they are investors hiding behind a generic email address, trying to flip the name for wholesale. It's important we exclude those people from our prospects list because we can find bigger fish.

When you've done this as long as I have, you start to recognize their addresses. Plus, they tend to use copy-and-paste style email templates, which is a dead giveaway they are not the best buyer. Some of these templates employ some common lies to prey upon your sympathies. They'll say, "I'm a broke college student looking to start up a business," or "I'm a starving entrepreneur and getting a break on this domain would be a huge help." These same stories have been circulating in inquiry emails to the point of being a worn-out trope in our industry. They might be better off going to a creative writing class to come up with some new material!

You should also show extreme caution when someone reaches out and says, "Just name your price." The people who send these kinds of inquiries about your domain name do so because they know it works. But if you don't have the experience at pricing—or getting multiple offers in play—then you could be doing yourself a disservice by under-selling.

It's important to note how some of these incognito offers could actually be serious contenders. While the email might say it's from Bob_The_Big_Nobody@gmail.com, it may turn out to be CEO Bob at a Fortune 500—or it could be Bob the Successful Serial Entrepreneur who is about to launch his next big startup. Naturally, he's not going to use the company email address and blow his cover—but that's exactly who you want to attract as a buyer!

Which is why you want to save every email you ever receive about your domain name. Now, I know what you're thinking:

"But what if I've already deleted all those emails?"

You wouldn't be alone in doing so. Most people delete emails instead of archiving. So first, start archiving everything instead. They are priceless when it comes to helping you put together your list of prospects as well as hone in on the true value of your domain name.

As I mentioned before, the collection of emails also tells a story about who to market the name to. Even if there are some lowball, non-serious offers, we can see what type of people are interested in the name. Is it a specific industry? If so, then let's go find out who the big players are in that industry and see who else might want in on the action.

So even if an email looks like junk on the surface, it might be a mask for a very interesting prospect. I actually know the General Counsel of a major corporation who uses this exact strategy—he uses a bland-looking, non-corporate gmail account to reach out to domain owners and try to buy domain names. And his company owns a lot of solid, generic domain names because of this strategy.

Obviously, all this kind of filtering and analysis requires a ton of work. More importantly, it requires a higher level of experience to decipher the real offers from the fakers. Which is why we need to get into answering the question, "When should I hire a domain broker?"

CHAPTER 16

WHEN TO HIRE
A DOMAIN BROKER

RECENTLY, I HAD a client approach me who originally formed his business back in the 1970s. When he learned about domain names in the '90s, he went and got his and has held onto it ever since. For years now, he's received regular emails inquiring about whether he would consider selling the name, including some direct offers.

Like I mentioned in the last chapter, I asked him to forward me the emails he had saved—and thankfully, he had saved quite a few. In fact, when we went through his emails, we found one offer for $750,000 from *ten* years ago. With some investigating, I was able to see this was a real offer, which positioned him exceptionally well for a seven-figure deal if we decided to take the name to auction now.

Back in Chapter 12, we talked about when to hire a domain broker if you're looking to buy, but it looks entirely different when you're looking to sell. If you have a low-value domain name, that is, under five figures, you really don't need a broker's help other than maybe reaching out to ask for some quick advice. You can probably skip ahead to Chapter 13 and consider some of the marketplaces available, including auction sites.

But if your domain name passes the Premium Test, it's a different story. When you have that one-word, easy-to-spell .COM that was originally registered before the year 2000, you're going to want to take more caution. Based on the trends, you're looking at bigger money, which automatically means a more complicated transaction.

But let's get into some of the "signals" you should look for.

SIGNAL #1: YOU'RE READY TO SELL

This one can be complicated because only you can decide if you're ready to sell. Given the emotional attachment you might have to a certain domain name, it's not surprising if you can't put a dollar value on it.

A while ago, an older gentleman reached out to me about selling some of his high-value domain names. This individual was very much a pioneer in the digital age and you could count him among the people who invented the internet. He had been using computers before most of the world and was the original registrant for a particularly premium domain name. In fact, he'd had the name for so long, he had registered it by *writing* in to request the name.

Unfortunately, he had received a terrible prognosis from his doctor—and the clock was running. Knowing what he had on his hands, he didn't want his family to have to deal with the digital assets after he passed. He'd known of Brannans by reputation and trusted we would be able to help him sell the domain for as much as possible, which could then go to his estate or any medical costs the family would be left with.

Let me be direct here—don't sell until you're ready. I know that sounds surprising coming from a broker, but I absolutely believe in it. Never let someone strong arm you into a deal or guilt you into selling because you're "not using it."

At the same time, don't wait too long either. I'm grateful this gentleman reached out to me the way he did because I've also dealt with plenty of other cases where the family is having to deal with the digital assets and aren't sure what to do. Sometimes they can end up selling it for too low to an investor because they don't know what they have on their hands. A broker's job is always to make sure you get the most possible, period.

SIGNAL #2: YOU GET AN EMAIL FROM MARKMONITOR, CSC, OR MARKSMEN

The more premium your name, the more emails you'll get. Which is why you need to save them all. But you especially need to pay attention if you get an email from MarkMonitor, CSC, or Marksmen. A quick overview of who they are:

MarkMonitor: Founded in 1999, they have developed software specifically for protecting brands from bad actors—including fraud, cybersquatting, IP violations, piracy, and even digital counterfeiting.

CSC: Founded way back in 1899, CSC has long been a leader in corporate legal protection and tax services. With the rise of the internet and digital IP, they consistently work with brands on protecting their brand identities through domain names.

Marksmen: Smaller than the other two, Marksmen is still important to know because they provide extensive IP protection services, which can include domain acquisitions, trademark investigations, and even securing social media handles.

In some form or fashion, all three operate as brand protection agencies, working with companies to secure digital assets like domain names. Typically, they are working with bigger companies—so it can be a great indicator that you have one of the "big dogs" coming to the table.

For instance, it's unlikely you will receive a direct email from a company like Verizon, Apple, or Ford. Instead, they hire these companies to manage their IP and when they want a domain name, they typically have these companies reach out and gauge interest. Usually it's because they have some kind of new product or service they're developing and in the interest of the brand and marketing campaign, your domain name has caught their eye.

Granted, it could also be a startup behind the outreach. Perhaps they just got an injection of venture capital funding so they can upgrade their name to a more desirable domain. In Section V: Case Studies, you'll see just how common this is among brands, whether they are hundred-year-old corporations or one-year-old startups.

While it can still be a good sign if you're receiving other unsolicited emails, the ones you receive from these three specific sources indicate a higher level of legitimacy. It should make you go back through any other offer emails and see if there are other legitimate ones hiding in there. Exactly when you should have an experienced broker lend a trained eye.

Even if you're not quite ready to sell yet, you should still use this as a sign to reach out to a broker and ask questions. Most of us are comfortable with at least doing an initial consultation to see how you would like to proceed—or whether it's worth reaching back out to see what kind of offer they have in mind. If nothing else, this can help you establish the baseline for valuation for whenever you *are* ready to sell.

SIGNAL #3: YOUR DOMAIN NAME HAS BROAD APPEAL

In the last chapter, we discussed how sometimes a certain domain name is of interest to a single industry or niche—like Christian.com. But every now and then, a name comes along which actually transcends multiple industry sectors because of its broad appeal . . . which means things can get *really* interesting!

One time I was approached by such a client who realized the domain name on his hands could be of interest to a myriad of companies in completely different sectors. Instead of going the route of narrowing down a few interested buyers, it made sense for him to go to auction—so he definitely needed broker support.

Domain name auctions can be just as high-energy as a live auction. The name ended up in a bidding war, which meant I spent the entire day on the phone, going back-and-forth between two companies—one was a bank and the other was a computer company. Like I said, multiple sectors.

The bank even held an emergency board meeting on the day of the auction to discuss how high they were willing to go. They called me up and said, "This is our final offer, so if the other party wins but the deal falls through, let us know." For the record, if you work at a massive corporation, I personally consider this a bad negotiating strategy. Very few win-win negotiations get everyone to the table with this "best and final" approach.

In the end, though, it was a dark horse who came out of the blue and won the auction—a moving company! Talk about a domain name with broad appeal.

The seller was overjoyed with how the transaction went, feeling like he had gotten away with something—and the buyer was excited they had both the .COM and an EMD (exact match domain) to boost their brand identity.

WORKING TOGETHER

Ultimately, you want all three of these signals working together—you want to be ready to sell, receive interesting unsolicited offers from legitimate sources, and have a name with broad enough appeal that you're not considering just one buyer. Just like basic economics teaches us, higher demand will always drive the price up—and when you have a premium domain name, the supply is automatically as limited as it can be! Supply = one. Because for every word in the English language, there is only one exact match .COM domain for that word.

So once you have at least one of these signals, it's time to reach out to a broker and ask what it looks like to work together on a sale. For my part, I always like to walk people through the process and make sure they have a clear understanding on what will happen at each step—and what resources are available to move the sale forward.

CHAPTER 17

DOMAIN NAME RESOURCES

J UST LIKE IN any industry, you need resources to make it work. And while I've mentioned various resources throughout the book, I want to focus our attention here specifically on those you should know about when you are getting ready to sell a premium domain name.

Some of these resources, especially the marketplaces, can come in handy even if you don't have a premium domain name. If you're interested in the investing side of the industry and just want to flip names for a few thousand dollars, then you'll also want to become familiar with some of the resources mentioned here.

DOMAIN NAME MARKETPLACES

When it comes to where to buy a domain name, there's really no shortage of places to look. But to keep you from being overwhelmed, here's a solid shortlist you can refer to:

- Atom
- GoDaddy / Afternic / Dan
- HugeDomains
- Flippa
- Sedo
- BrandBucket

Atom (formerly Squadhelp) helps people find great names for their brands, websites, and products. They use AI-powered tools plus ideas from creative people around the world to come up with unique and catchy names. Their service also checks if domain names are available, making it easier for users to find the perfect fit for their needs.

Not many people create companies as a direct result of their dissertation—but that's exactly what German doctoral student Tim Schumacher did. In 1999, he wrote a thesis where he specifically referenced the lack of an online domain name marketplace.

Along with his partners Ulrich Prisoner, Ulrich Essmann, and Marius Würzner, they started up Sedo in 2001. Sedo, which is short for Search Engine for Domain Offers, became one of the first online marketplace for buying, selling, and parking domain names. According to ICANNWiki, they maintain the world's largest domain distribution network, known as SedoMLS—which is another reminder of how much the industry shares with real estate.

By no means have they remained the only marketplace. GoDaddy has become the largest marketplace, especially when you consider that the marketplaces Afternic and Dan.com are now both a part of the "GoDaddy family." Even so, the user experience on their platforms is different with various features, so it's definitely not a one-size-fits-all experience.

HugeDomains is another marketplace of note, as it certainly lives up to its name with over a million domain names for sale. And another I should mention is Flippa.com, which not only allows you to buy and sell the domain names, but also has an option to sell a fully developed website. For example, if someone wanted to offload an e-commerce brand they had started, they could sell the entire business through Flippa.

I've used Flippa myself in the past to sell half a million worth of domain names. But one caveat—when I used it they did not require KYC (Know Your Customer) procedures. That is, they did not require users to provide basic qualifying information like on other platforms. So you would find twelve-year-olds getting on and bidding for fun, winning the bid, and then unable to pay . . . which becomes very frustrating to say the least!

Last but not least, there is also BrandBucket which I mentioned back in Chapter 9 because of how it's geared to help founders identify strong brands. But if you own a premium name which could make for a great brand name, it's definitely one to be aware of.

AUCTIONS

Beyond the marketplaces, you'll also find the auction sites. When I first started in the industry, auctions were largely our bread and butter—which is why Brannans has started our own auction site to help streamline the bidding process for our customers. Live auctions of domain names still exist, usually in conjunction with conferences, but as far as the online marketplace goes, here are a few key ones to know about:

- Brannans
- ROTD
- Flippa
- GoDaddy / Afternic / Dan
- Namecheap
- Efty (designed with investors in mind)
- Sedo

While I provided this list back in Chapter 11 for buyers, sellers also need to know what options are available for taking your name to auction—even when you have a broker assisting you.

Of course, GoDaddy's auction service is probably the most robust since it has additional offerings like name renewal services and even website building and hosting. Efty is another service to at least know about, though it wouldn't be my top choice when it comes to selling a premium domain name since it's aimed more for investors. Still, if you're selling without the help of a broker and need to liquidate quickly, it could be a good option for you.

DOMAIN NAME MANAGEMENT

Whether you have one domain name or a whole portfolio, having them all under a domain name management service is vital for security—especially when you have some premium names in the mix. Once again, you'll find some of the usual suspects among the registrars:

- Bluehost
- DreamHost
- Dynadot
- GoDaddy
- Hover
- Hostinger

- IONOS
- Namecheap

Remember, as a best practice, you don't want your domain names to be spread out among multiple registrars. It's always best if you move your entire portfolio together under one roof, both for keeping your life easier and more secure.

TRANSACTIONS

When it comes to the actual transaction process of selling a domain name, you really only need to know about one resource—Escrow.com. Simply put, do not buy or sell a domain name without using Escrow. com.

They are the global gold standard for secure transactions. They've never lost a dollar or a domain name in the process of moving the registration from one owner to another. The only thing they can't do is prevent you from buying a stolen name. On that particular front, you still need to do your due diligence to make sure you're buying the name from the registrant. But keep in mind that in a case of a stolen domain name, the registrant information has been changed by the thief.

Still, at minimum, Escrow.com is able to guarantee ID verification for you and your company in terms of the person you're dealing with. They follow KYC (Know Your Customer) procedures for verification, including federal laws, and AML (Anti-Money Laundering) regulations set out by the Office of Foreign Assets Control (OFAC).

Given the international nature of the business, OFAC regulations are particularly important because they prevent you from accepting or sending money from somewhere you're not supposed to. So Escrow.com is a great safeguard that protects you from sending money to an embargoed country like Iran or to a terrorist cell.

Back in the day, if you were selling a domain name, you couldn't be sure of who the buyer truly was. Given all the variables in the online world, they could be a terrorist hiding out in Iran but using a UK bank account to try to circumvent legal barriers. Escrow.com's setup makes transactions safe so you don't get a knock on the door from people in suits.

Escrow.com has secured over six billion dollars of transactions for everything from vintage cars, collector guitars, jewelry—you name it. But they got started with domain names and are used by almost everyone in the industry. Their tagline is "Never buy and sell online without using Escrow.com," but it's more than just a slogan—it's the truth.

SEARCH TOOLS FOR IDENTIFYING PROSPECTIVE BUYERS

When you're selling a domain name, the search process is different than buying. What you're really doing is searching to identify the best prospective buyers.

For example, let's say that I'm looking to sell a certain domain name like Batteries.com. As a broker, my job is to find the right buyers to come to the table, so I should search to see who else owns related domain names, like Batteries.net, Batteries.fr, or Batteries.jp. By searching the WHOIS records, I can identify some warm prospects to get the best price possible.

As you might already assume, GoDaddy is the de facto search engine for words, but there are several others which you should know about:

- DomainIQ
- DomainTools
- DomainIndex

DomainIQ and DomainTools both have historical lookup features so you can see transaction history—at least, what's publicly available. My personal favorite is DomainIQ because it's cheaper when searching for names at scale, especially when I need to do a WHOIS search on the ownership history for the name.

Another tool I use regularly with searches is URL Opener, which allows me to open up ten tabs at the same time. I can then use it to automatically create a spreadsheet rather than tediously having to copy-paste all the information myself. I can typically do fifty to two hundred names with corresponding data at a time, allowing me to quickly identify potential buyers.

LinkedIn is another great search tool when scoping prospective buyers. I can easily find brand matches for a domain and see how many employees each of those companies has. With this data, the client and I can gain a better picture on who will be able to make the best offer.

Crunchbase is another tool which allows me to identify the "big fish" to go after. Their pro version allows me to search up to a hundred decision makers a month, including verifying their contact info. Then I'm able to reach out and let them know about the domain name being offered for sale. When coupled with URL Opener, I can quickly find brand-match companies who are publicly-traded and, therefore, the best prospects.

AI has quickly become valuable in all things. I've been using Chat.com a lot more than Google these days, and I find the quality of the search results to be much better. Some of my own go-tos have been:

- Chat.com
- Gemini.Google.com
- Grok.com
- Claude.com

(If you're a big fan of AI, take a look at Imarena Chatbot Arena's Leaderboard at: *https://lmarena.ai/?leaderboard*.)

Everything mentioned here are also great CYA tools during the selling process. That is, if I'm able to show that I'm marketing the domain name to multiple companies, it takes away any kind of legal argument that the seller is trying to take advantage of a single brand and their trademark.

For instance, let's pretend you own Clements.com and want to sell it. If you only reach out to one company—Clements Computers—then it comes across to them like you're holding the name "hostage" and infringing on their brand. But if you can show that you've also reached out to Clements Moving Company, Clements Automotive, Clements

Grills & Smokers, and Clements Talent Agency, then it's proof that you're simply seeking out any interested parties.

And as you might recall from the story from the last chapter, you never know when a "dark horse" contender may come forward as the top bidder. It's always good to keep your options open—and you can only do so if your broker is utilizing search tools to find you the best options.

DOMAIN NAME ATTORNEYS

It's one thing to be an IP attorney—it's a whole other thing to be an IP attorney who specializes in domain names. If you haven't done so already, you might consider revisiting this topic we covered back in Chapter 6. So let's look closer at when you want to have a domain name attorney in your corner.

One of the biggest concerns of individual domain owners is getting sued by a corporation over their name. The story of Uzi Nissan is incredibly relevant on this point.

Uzi Nissan owned the domain name Nissan.com simply because it was his last name—and he had done so before Nissan Motors ever thought to. Over the years, Nissan Motors kept trying to sue him to get the name away from him, saying it should be theirs because of their trademark.

He spent over $3 million having to defend his own last name from the company because he had no interest in selling it to them. Unfortunately, after he died, someone at the registrar decided to be shady—and transferred Nissan.com to Nissan Motors without an official transaction. The family then had to fight to get the name back—which thankfully, they did—thanks to the work by their domain name attorney.[56] Now, if Nissan Motors ever wants to legitimately own the name, they'll have to pay dearly for it—probably in the tens of millions. You might consider this a "grudge tax" for what they pulled but the simple fact is that the domain name Nissan.com is not for sale.

When you have registered a domain name that is a generic term—or your name like in the case of Uzi Nissan—you have rights to it as the registrant which can supersede a trademark. Still, it won't stop some jerk from trying to come after you, thinking they can get a trademark to take it away.

In my career, I've had to talk people off the ledge from giving in to this kind of trademark bullying. While I can offer some advice, the ultimate conversation needs to be between them and a qualified domain name attorney—someone who has defended hundreds of WIPO cases (The World Intellectual Property Organization), not just for general IP or trademark issues, but specific to domain names. See Chapter 3 for a list of some of my go-to recommendations.

Domain name attorneys truly are the unsung heroes in the industry. If you have a name under your belt which could invite a trademark dispute, you'll want to make sure you have a domain name attorney in your corner who can fight for you so you don't lose what is rightfully yours.

YOUR ULTIMATE RESOURCE

This is a ton of information to keep up with, I know. This industry can be incredibly rewarding, but it's also incredibly complicated. Which is why I decided to write this book. I certainly don't have all of the answers. When I'm stuck and need information, I use the resources listed in the book to find it.

We live in a world of fast and frequent change—including the resources available to you. Recognizing that fact, I want to end this chapter with a small caveat. The information here is purely based on my best recommendations at the time of printing. However, you can find an up-to-date list of various domain name resources on our website, Brannans.com, as well as sign up for our newsletter to receive industry updates.

Once you have your resources lined up, you can embark on the process of actually selling your premium domain name. So let's explore what the process looks like, step-by-step.

CHAPTER 18

SELLING A PREMIUM DOMAIN NAME

IF YOU'VE EVER been to a vineyard, then you know a lot more goes into the process of wine-making than simply squashing grapes and storing the juice. The real magic happens long before the grapes are even harvested. Today's greatest wineries are using techniques that have been honed from literally thousands of years of wine making, all so you can enjoy some vino at your next client dinner—or while making the toast at your child's wedding.

Great wine takes years to make, of course. And the last thing any winemaker wants to do is spend years cultivating their distinctive, premium blend—only to have it spill all over the roadway when it comes time to deliver.

Selling a premium domain name is similar. Like wine, it grows in flavor over time, becoming more valuable, more rich and more profitable for the owner. So when it comes time to sell, you want to make sure it's going to be put to good use—and of course, that you get top dollar for it.

When it comes to selling a premium domain name owned by an individual, I see two main stories time after time. One common scenario is that the original registrant knows how valuable the name is—if for no other reason they have been telling people "No" for twenty-five years. And now, they're coming to me because they're finally ready to sell it but want to make sure it's done correctly.

Another common scenario is due to the death of a loved one who had the registration. The story I hear from administrators and executors is often the same: "They kept telling me this was really valuable, but I just don't know what to believe."

But once the idea of selling your domain name comes to mind, what should you do? What are the steps you need to take?

STEP 1: CONFIRM YOU HAVE A PREMIUM NAME

We've already covered how to measure whether you have a premium domain name on your hands, so go back to Chapter 15 if you need to and conduct the Premium Test:

- Is it a one-word .COM?
- Was it registered before 2000?
- Is the SLD easy to spell/correctly spelled?

If you're still not certain, you can reach out to myself or another established, experienced broker to get our input. Even if you haven't enlisted the broker's help yet, you can certainly ask them what they might be able to sell it for. When you speak to brokers, please get an NDA in place and make it clear to them that you do not authorize them to speak to anyone else about your domain name. As I've mentioned previously, some people will front-run a domain name that they don't have an engagement for just to see if they can insert themselves into the middle of a transaction for a piece of the pie.

Also, beware of the Anchoring Effect! Once a broker tells you a number, it's going to be hard for you to get that number out of your head—just like that pesky sticker on a car windshield. Which brings us to a giant caveat—even as experienced as I am in this field, my guess at the value is still just that—a *guess*. Generally, I tell people "We don't appraise names," because I know that I'll be making the number up.

You have to consider what the name is worth to you—what the lowest offer you're willing to consider is—as well as what the best buyer will be able to offer. If you're a high-net worth individual, then you have a lot more say in the valuation. Now, that doesn't mean you get to say "I want $50 million" for a name that's probably only worth $100K. At a certain point, market demand has to be considered, too.

Michael Saylor, CEO of MicroStrategy, famously sold Voice.com for a record-breaking $30 million in 2019. During the negotiation process, he actually rejected $22 million. If you or your company has a one-word .COM domain name and you're offered $22 million for it, would you reject it? Or would you tell your CEO to reject it on the off chance that the buyer would come to $30 million? Likely not, but I do know a few people who would do just that. My guess is that the Nissan family would reject $22 million from the Nissan Motor Company.

If there is a large disparity between what you want to sell it for and what the market is offering, it could indicate you are overvaluing it. But it could also mean it's not the right time to sell—or that you haven't found the right buyer yet.

It's nearly impossible to truly value a name *before* you market it. As we've addressed, you can get a rough idea of a starting line if you've saved emails that had explicit offers in them. But even so, these are a guide for where to start, not the final price, because the name will likely have accrued value since then.

STEP 2: SECURE THE DOMAIN NAME

Once the name's premium status is established, the next move you should make is to ensure the domain is secure. Make sure that the password you use for the domain name is unique and only used for that one thing. If you fail to take this security step, you may not have a premium domain name on your hands for long.

As terrible as it sounds, you'll find bad actors out in the world who target domain names registered to the recently deceased. And they will actively work to hack the account to steal the registration for themselves.

I've seen this exact situation happen. A widow near Boston had inherited a domain name as part of her husband's estate, and it was about as premium a name as you could hope for. My best guess is it would have fetched at least $10 million at auction, if not more.

So as I've touched on in other chapters, you will want to make sure you are enlisting protection services through your registrar. This can mean locking in the max time for domain name renewal (five to ten years) and using a generic email address that multiple people can have access to so you don't get frozen out of the account (if it's a corporate owned domain).

This is especially true when a corporation discovers they have a premium domain name on their hands that they aren't using and they need to liquidate. If that's you, then someone needs to be tasked to find out how much the name is worth by following these same steps. Unfortunately, many small and medium-sized businesses don't do this step. They've had the same person handling the domain names for two decades—and now that person has one foot out the door.

Instead, transfer the registration to the generic email (Example: Domains@CompanyName.com), and make sure multiple people have access to those emails so they see any notice that the registrar sends about the status of their domain(s). Even if you're not a corporation, it's still a best practice to make sure your administrator or executor knows how to access your emails and the account at your registrar.

You might be wondering, "How do we transfer the registration, though?"

Now, you can look at this as a sales pitch for GoDaddy all you want to—but I've found that transferring the domain name registration over to GoDaddy is the best move you can make for the security of the domain name. In fact, when I spoke with David Weslow, the domain name IP attorney, for this book, I put him on the spot and asked him what site he considers the most secure—and he didn't skip a beat to say GoDaddy.

At Brannans, we've made this a best practice with our clients—when preparing to sell the domain name, we advise them to move it to GoDaddy before we start marketing the name for sale. Not a knock against the others out there, and I'm sure other brokers have their preferences.

Getting the domain name transferred is pretty easy. Once upon a time, you had to complete physical paperwork which slowed down the process, but now everything is done digitally with an authorization code.

Now, an important note here—only the domain owner can request the authorization code to make the transfer happen from the original registrar to GoDaddy. A broker cannot do it. However, when I'm working with a client, I'm happy to walk them through the process.

STEP 3: PICK A DOMAIN NAME BROKER

Maybe this one was too obvious, but it has to be said! If you want to make sure you get the best buyers who will offer top dollar through a secure, legal transaction—then you'll need a broker.

Similar to a real estate agent, a talent agent, or even a damages lawyer, a legitimate broker doesn't get paid unless you do. While there are no industry standards for the commissions we take, you'll find anything between 10 percent to 25 percent of the final sale price. For our part, as of November 2024, for brokerage we have a fixed fee of 15 percent, and for acquisition it's 15 percent or $2,500, whichever is greater. That said, if you have a budget that's in the $10,000+ range, we'd love to speak with you.

When you have a domain broker in your corner, the process will not only go so much smoother, but you stand a much better chance of getting the best buyers to the table.

Which is exactly why you want someone who has experience with international transactions. It's never a guarantee your buyer will be based in the US—I've seen top bidders come from Australia, Germany, China, and the UK, to name a few. So you want someone who has their pulse on the industry enough to effectively negotiate across cultural and language barriers.

Once you have your domain name broker selected, they will take the reins on marketing the name and finding you the best price. After all, it's in their own best interest to do so. They're going to start a spreadsheet and begin the process of identifying dozens if not hundreds of potential buyers.

As mentioned back in Chapter 16 and 17, brokers will utilize all the resources at their disposal to identify the best prospects for your name. This includes looking for exact match companies who would benefit from upgrading their domain name but can also include finding industry niches who would take an interest in your name.

By marketing the name, it builds buzz and traction for the eventual sale, whether you end up deciding to negotiate one-on-one with a buyer or take the name to auction for a bidding war.

So if you haven't already picked a broker by this point, this is the last call to do so. The next steps can prove tricky if you're on your own.

STEP 4(A): THE NEGOTIATION

In Chapter 11, I told the story of negotiating the sale of Frida.com from the original registrant to the baby goods company Frida. In that situation, I was representing the buyer, of course—but it's a great illustration for a seller who decides to deal one-on-one with a prospective buyer.

After all, FridaBaby was not the only company who had made an offer over the years—the seller could have taken it to auction. But in the end, heading to the negotiation table gave the seller the highest sense of control in the situation.

I've always loved the negotiation process from a business standpoint—but I love it from a personal one, too. One of my favorite parts of the job is when everyone at the negotiation table leaves feeling like they won.

Before moving on, though, it should be mentioned that the negotiation is about more than just the final price. The money is only one piece of the puzzle. Other details have to be negotiated, such as the when, how the name is going to be used, who will be using it, and so on. For instance, a seller may want to stipulate that the buyer won't turn around and sell the name for a certain amount of time—or use it for a product/service the seller has a morality problem with.

You might recall with the Frida sale, one of the terms we negotiated was that the seller would have emails forwarded for several months after the transaction because they had been using it as the domain for their email server. It's these types of details where an experienced domain broker can help make sure all the I's are dotted and the T's crossed.

STEP 4(B): THE AUCTION

We don't need to recycle everything about actions from Chapter 17, but it's worth mentioning that a broker can provide invaluable support in this process. The key to making the auction a success is communicating—making sure you have done the legwork to market the domain name to the right people to come to the table at the right time.

You never want to leave money on the table because you failed to get the attention of the best prospects. Brokers will perform thorough searches and outreach to prospective buyers. This is where you also want to make sure you have a broker who is comfortable with reaching out and communicating with corporate types—the C-Suite, General Counsels, or even the heads of marketing or IP. If you don't know how to get their attention, then you might not be getting the best people to the auction.

With their in-depth knowledge of the industry and which auctions are best suited for your specific domain name, this is where you need to let the broker take the lead. So long as the broker is putting your needs first to make sure you get the best possible deal, then let them do what they need to do to get the auction set up.

And then when the day comes, hold onto your hats and be ready for a wild ride. It can become quite the frenzy once you've got the highest-paying prospects in the room—even when it's a digital room.

STEP 5: ESCROW AND TRANSFER AGREEMENT

Whether you negotiate with one party or go to auction, eventually you'll have to go through the escrow and transfer agreement process. How long this step takes often depends on who you're actually selling to. A startup can move more quickly because their organizational structure is flatter. An established, large corporation will have more steps in the process, and they may need a little more time to go over everything and get the necessary approvals from everyone in the decision-making process.

Having done this for so long and working with some of the best domain name attorneys in the world, I've built up a repertoire of standard agreements that can be used in the domain transfer process. From there, it's a round or two of redlines and comments until everyone agrees on the language then signs (digitally) on the dotted line.

Once this happens, the transaction is set up at Escrow.com. Just like any major property transfer, it's a necessary move to make sure both the money and property end up in the right hands. Escrow.com ends up making sure the seller and broker get paid—and that the buyer has the domain name.

Once Escrow.com confirms that the transfer of both money and domain name have happened, the deal is done—and everyone gets something they wanted. You as the seller have the money you can use as you like, the buyer has a domain name to boost their brand, and your broker can add another notch to their belt.

OWNER FINANCING AS A SELLING STRATEGY

Back in Chapter 13, we covered the advantages of financing a premium domain name from the buyer's perspective, but what about for you as a seller? How could this help you out?

First, not everyone can offer owner financing. If you need to liquidate quickly for some reason, then setting up an installment agreement with a buyer probably isn't going to be of interest. But if you're open to a longer-term arrangement which poses very little risk for you as a seller, then it's definitely an interesting possibility.

For starters, financing the sale of the domain name opens up your buyer market more. The person who values your domain name the most isn't always the person with the most cash. This could be the founder of a startup who is still trying to close a funding round but recognizes how the exact match domain name would boost their profile and maybe even help them close the round.

In my experience, these scrappy founders will give up just about anything before they default on their payment. It's incredibly rare for a financing arrangement for a premium name to fall through.

Second, you don't have to take many extra steps to the process described above. In fact, Escrow.com already has a holding transaction option to secure a financing deal. It includes some standard fees, plus an additional $25 a month for the length the term, so it's not a tremendous cost to add in. And what's great about Escrow is they will honor any agreement between you and the buyer—they're not going to come in and change up the language, forcing you to do something you don't want. Also, in the event your family later comes along and says, "We want to revoke this agreement," they can't do it. Escrow will continue to uphold the arrangement between you and the buyer.

Third, you can make more money over the long term because you can set up a charge of 10 to 15 percent interest. You could even choose to see this more like an investment, considering this rate yields you a better return than many traditional investment strategies. There may also be tax benefits to a longer term. For that, you'd need to speak to your accountant or financial advisor.

And finally, there's very little risk to you. The way the deal works is that Escrow.com serves as an intermediary during the course of the financing agreement. Escrow technically holds the domain name's registration—not the buyer who is financing. The buyer is able to functionally use it as though it were completely in their name, though, in the same way you are completely able to use a car or house you buy through financing. And then once all the payments have been made to close out the arrangement, the registration is fully transferred from Escrow to the buyer.

But let's say the buyer defaults on their payments. At this point, Escrow terminates the agreement and reverts the registration back to you, the seller. You keep everything you've already been paid *and* you have the asset back in your name. Which means you get the chance to sell it again if you want to.

I actually know someone who has done a financing agreement on one of his domains where it defaulted twice, so now he's able to sell it for a third time. He considers it one of his most valuable investments ever, considering what he's made from it.

Sometimes people are concerned about this last point: "What if I can't resell the name again because the buyer tarnished the name before defaulting?" While this could possibly happen, it's very unlikely. If it's a premium name, any buyer would be foolish to damage their ranking. They don't have any motivation for damaging the SEO on the name. This separates it from the world of real estate where someone who is being foreclosed on intentionally damages the property to make it more difficult for the bank to resell.

Like with other transactions, we've done so many of these, we've developed a boilerplate template agreement for clients to use if they decide to go the financing route. As with any buying agreement, the seller still gets to set specific terms, such as a morality clause. This is especially important for a corporation or an individual who still has an emotional attachment to the name. You don't necessarily want to see it end up with a website promoting adult content, gambling, or some other activity that violates your morals.

So with little risk to you the seller, offering owner financing has very few drawbacks. In fact, financing the sale can actually help you spread out your tax liability instead of taking the hit all in one year. Financing the sale to the buyer can actually keep you from crossing over into a new tax bracket—just in case you need an incentive.

Still, some sellers want to be done with the name and have it off their plate. So if you find a buyer who can pay cash in full, it's not my job as a broker to push anyone into a financing arrangement. But if you want to bring the most people to the table, owner financing is a creative strategy to make even more from the sale than you may have initially thought you could.

STRATEGIC DOMAIN NAME TRANSACTIONS

Remember, there are many reasons a buyer may want your premium domain name—they may be looking to upgrade their brand, release a new product, or launch the next game-changing startup. Especially in the case of the startup scenario, they may not have the funding yet to make an attractive offer. But what if they approach you with a modest amount of cash and a piece of equity in the startup in exchange for the domain name?

I'll put it this way: If you're approached by a few former Google engineers about their startup idea, take the meeting.

I had a friend approached by a few former Google engineers with this very proposition. He took the meeting and made a deal with them for a token amount of cash and some equity in their startup. The company sold for more than $1 billion a few years later.

I don't know what the equity percentage was, but I do know that this individual had previously sold a domain name for $20 million (which isn't reported anywhere), and he told me that this one trans-action was the biggest he's ever had of all his domain name deals. Now that's what I'd call a strategic transaction!

CHAPTER 19

MITIGATING UDRP RISKS AND PROTECTING YOUR ASSETS

HERE ARE GENERALLY two ways to sell a domain name. The first of these is inbound—that is, you wait for an interested party to decide they'd like to buy whichever domain name you own and reach out to initiate the process of a potential sale. There's nothing wrong with this, but it's not always the most reliable method to sell a domain. Sometimes, people don't know what they want until they see it right in front of them.

I once read that Einstein could be teaching a lecture right now, but to a completely empty classroom. Why? Because nobody would know it was happening! With an increasing number of demands on our attention at any given moment, you can't expect people to know what they want without being made aware of it first. That's where the importance of outbound marketing comes in.

Outbound marketing is the second avenue you can take when it comes to selling your domain name. This means that rather than waiting for the right buyer to come to you, you instead actively contact individuals or corporations that you believe might be interested in buying the domain. Most domain brokers opt for this route when they have a high-value domain to sell—and there's nothing wrong with that.

After all, they have a job to do and any broker worth their commission fee will have the right connections and negotiation tactics to make outbound marketing a strong indicator of success. But I rarely see discussion about the risks involved with taking this route, especially when the domain in question includes a term of limited usage.

Enter: UDRP.

If you're planning on selling a domain name, having a strong understanding of UDRP is crucial. UDRP—or the Uniform Domain Name

Dispute Resolution Policy process—is something few domain brokers are aware of. Unfortunately, inexperienced brokers can get their clients into a legal shitstorm that might actually lose them their domain name. Briefing yourself on the UDRP process can help prevent potential problems arising later down the line—problems that may end up costing thousands of dollars in attorney fees to resolve at best, and lose your domain name at worst.

What is UDRP?

UDRP is all about who holds the rights to a domain name. When ICANN was first established, one of their biggest priorities was figuring out "The Trademark Dilemma." In other words, dealing with disputes regarding the use of trademarks as domain names in the absence of the trademark owner's consent.

In the late 1990s, an intellectual property case in the United Kingdom, British Telecommunications plc v One in a Million Ltd, served as a landmark ruling for laying the foundations of the UDRP process we know of today. In that case, the judge ruled that domain names who used a trademarked name without consent were "an instrument of fraud" and were at high risk of misleading consumers.

Soon after, the United Nations World Intellectual Property Organization began work on a report that set out the current three-stage test of the UDRP. This report recommended the creation of a procedure that would help resolve trademark disputes with domain names, and make it mandatory that each domain name application would be required to submit to the procedure if a claim was initiated against it by a third party. By December 1999, UDRP was born—fully outlining the procedural requirements for each stage of the dispute resolution process.

The first case determined under the new regulations involved the domain name WorldWrestlingFederation.com. (They now use the upgraded domain name, WWE.com.) If a business or organization thinks someone is holding a domain name in contravention of the UDRP, they can file a claim as the complainant. It usually costs around $1,000-2,000, depending on the number of domain names involved and whether the case will be decided by a panel of one or three. Here, there was only one domain name under dispute (WorldWrestlingFederation.com) filed by the complainant, the World Wrestling Federation.

The UDRP demands that a complainant prove each of the following three criteria are met in a case:

1. The domain name in question must be identical or confusingly similar to a trademark or service mark in which the complainant has rights.
2. The respondent has no legitimate interests in respect of the domain name.
3. The domain name has been registered and used in bad faith.

It was clear that the domain name WorldWrestlingFederation.com was identical or confusingly similar to the trademark and service mark used by the complainant (the World Wrestling Federation). It was also proven that the respondent, Michael Bosman, had no rights or legitimate interests in the domain name.

Here's where things get interesting: The complainant was able to prove that the domain name had been registered in bad faith. Only three days after it had been registered, Bosman offered to sell it to the World Wrestling Federation. But the criteria stipulate a name must have been registered and used in bad faith. Bosman hadn't built a website on the domain, so you could argue he hadn't actually used it.

However, the policy accounts for this and classes use as selling, renting or transferring the domain name registration to the complainant for "valuable consideration in excess of the documented out-of-pocket costs directly related to the domain name." Emphasis on the "in excess of" since Bosman had offered to sell the domain name to the World Wrestling Federation for more than the out-of-pocket costs directly related to the domain name, he had indeed "used" the domain name in bad faith as defined in the UDRP.

No surprises for guessing that the ruling did indeed go in favor of the complainant, and registration of the domain transferred over to the World Wrestling Federation.

BEST MEASURES

Some people, like Bosman, buy a domain name solely in the hopes that a bigger corporation will buy it back from them and they can make a tidy profit. If you reach out to a business and ask for their interest in buying a domain name that is similar to one of their trademarked terms, the panel have generally considered that to be strong evidence of bad faith.

But what about if you just don't know?

Unfortunately, many unsuspecting first-time sellers, investors and even unschooled brokers have been caught in an unintentional crossfire. Some end up in this situation because they don't realize that a trademark has been registered. Even if this is the case, a name can still have similar rights through business use. In certain countries like the US, Canada and Australia, trademark protection can be acquired simply through being used. Registration is not a necessary condition to warrant trademark protection, but is always advised to gain stronger legal protection and rights.

In any case, it's always a good idea to conduct a thorough Chat.com or Google search and look up the name on OpenCorporates.com to make sure it's not being used extensively by any one particular business. It's worth noting that UDRP doesn't only apply to .COM domain names, but in fact all generic top-level domains. That means you need to check out alternatives like .NET and .ORG as well as some country code top-level domains (ccTLDs) and even newer extensions like .XYZ and .ONLINE.

If your search results show that the name or term is being used by a variety of different organizations for different reasons, with none particularly dominating the results, it's still worth consulting with a domain lawyer before you breathe a sigh of relief. There are a number of attorneys specializing in intellectual property, domain names and UDRP who can give you adequate legal advice.

A particularly prominent lawyer in this space, John Berryhill, has some great advice for brokers or prospective sellers who want to embark on some outbound marketing for a domain name. He advises you to make it clear in your communications with prospective buyers that they're one of many potential parties being contacted about this domain. That way, a company won't feel like they're being singly targeted in bad faith. It's also a good sales technique to create urgency—and if your domain truly is a premium .COM then its value will be immediately apparent to the right buyer.

Berryhill also advises against domain registrants using "catch-all" sales or marketing emails to find potential leads. If a registrant knows that their domain is similar to a term used by another for communications and then finds themselves receiving misdirected emails, it could be grounds for a UDRP case. Past cases have seen registrants, for example, acquire a domain name, set up an email using that domain name and then demand an annual flat fee of thousands of dollars for any misdirected emails to be forwarded to the company for which they were intended.

In August 2020, a respondent contacted a complainant several times over LinkedIn, claiming they were receiving business emails concerning the other company and offering to sell the domain to them. The complainant declined, and the respondent essentially replied by saying, "imagine if this domain got into the hands of your competitors... they'd suddenly be privy to all of your private information."

In this case, the UDRP panel found it very likely that the domain was registered solely for the purpose of setting up a catch-all email address in the hope that emails intended for the prospective buyer would be misdirected to the registrant, allowing them to gain leverage over the complainant.

All this to say, be careful if you're a corporation. We always recommend businesses invest in a portfolio of domain names similar to their current domain that redirect back to the main website. It's not only great for marketing, but also a surefire way to protect yourself and your business from bad actors like the previous two examples.

THE DISPUTE PROCESS

When disputes do occur, the complainant will select an ICANN-approved administrative dispute resolution service provider who will administer the proceeding. These are usually categorized by location and include the following:

- The Arab Center for Dispute Resolution (ACDR)
- The Asian Domain Name Dispute Resolution Centre (ADNDRC)
- Canadian International Internet Dispute Resolution Centre (CIIDRC)
- Czech Arbitration Court, Arbitration Center for Internet Disputes (CAC)
- National Arbitration Forum (NAF)
- World Intellectual Property Organization (WIPO)

Proceedings will be carried out in accordance with the UDRP alongside any supplemental rules set forth by the service provider, but they were designed to be quicker, less expensive and more informal than traditional litigation. Another big benefit of UDRP is the fact that it's global – it's a single resolution process that can be used internationally, meaning a dispute can be resolved regardless of where the registrar, complainant or respondent are located.

Outcomes of a UDRP aren't always final, though. If a complainant loses the proceeding, they can still bring a lawsuit against the person who registered the domain name under local law, such as the Anti-Cybersquatting Consumer Protection Act, which would allow a US court of law to overturn a UDRP panel's decision if needed.

If an individual who has registered a domain name loses the rights to that name under a UDRP ruling, all is not lost for them, either. They can file a lawsuit against the trademark holder within ten business days, to prevent the registrar from transferring the domain name in the relevant jurisdiction (usually the registrant's location).

This is what happened in 2022, when Lamborghini S.p.A won the UDRP it filed against the domain Lambo.com. The domain registrant, Richard Blair, filed a lawsuit in response, claiming that he acquired the domain because he had been using the name Lambo as an alias in various online communities, and so it was not registered in bad faith against the company. His lawsuit stipulated, amongst other requests, that the registrar NameSilo, LLC was not to transfer the Lambo.com domain name over to Lamborghini.

Lamborghini tried to have the case dismissed, and Blair in turn tried to have Lamborghini sanctioned. Both attempts were unsuccessful, the case is still ongoing at the time of writing, and if you go to Lambo.com (as of November 2024) you'll see a for-sale landing page with an asking price of $75 million.

Ultimately, the guidance of an experienced domain lawyer can help prevent and overcome any issues pertaining to UDRP. I would highly recommend contacting John Berryhill or another attorney with a background in UDRP if you have any doubt about a domain name – after all, each case is unique and must be assessed appropriately.

CHAPTER 20

DOMAIN NAME CYBERSECURITY RISKS FOR COMPANIES

CYBERSECURITY IS A real threat for all of us—individuals and corporations alike. In the last chapter, I shared the story of the widow who had a domain name stolen from her by a cybercriminal. While we've touched on some of the security risks that everyone should consider, I can't close out this section of the book without addressing some specific threats for companies, big and small alike.

In fact, there's a chance you came to this book because your boss told you to figure out some of the domain names the company has acquired over time. Maybe the higher-ups want to see if there are any that can be offloaded to boost the bottom line and streamline systems.

So before you sell a domain name, you should know up front some of the cybersecurity risks facing companies—and some best practices to bring you more security.

PASSWORDS

The absolute biggest security risk related to owning a domain name is the password for the registered account. Companies sometimes fall into the trap of being so naive around cybersecurity, they use the same password from an email address for the registrar login. It may be the same exact password they used on a social media account, Netflix, or any other account that may have had a data leak—and now that the password is out on the dark web for people to find.

All it takes is for one bad actor to take the password, try it out with your domain registrar—and then suddenly they have access to your domain names. A few more clicks and they can transfer the registration over to themselves and that's that.

You have to take it seriously. Bad actors are everywhere, looking for vulnerabilities they can exploit and steal away your digital assets. So remember, just because you changed the password on one account over a security threat doesn't mean you did on the others.

Large companies with a CISO are often better at staying on top of these kinds of threats and establish rules around passwords and cybersecurity. Intercontinental Exchange (ICE) uses a security tool known as "Kraken" to enhance the security of their employees' emails. Kraken specifically focuses on monitoring and securing email communications. Everyone there is prepared as a result—it's just another way to keep cybersecurity front of mind and ensure they're protecting all of their assets, including information that their employees have access to.

But it's easy for smaller companies to overlook this detail in the daily grind. And yet, if you're at a small or medium-sized company, your domain name is still just as important to your brand. You don't want to wake up one day to find your domain being held ransom, your customers' data exposed, and your brand irrevocably tarnished.

Every account you set up in your company should have a different password. Can't remember them all? Me neither! Use a 1Password to keep track of them all—many browsers now have password managers built in, including Chrome and Safari.

SECURITY BEST PRACTICES

Skepticism can sometimes be your greatest ally in the world of cybersecurity. For instance, if a prospective buyer offers to pay in Bitcoin, there could be an initial temptation to say yes, especially given the long-term investment gains that Bitcoin is capable of.

Since bitcoin transfers are done on the blockchain, you might think, "It's secure because the blockchain is proof the coin is actually out there."

But the bitcoin offer could be a ruse to get you to click a link which then phishes your data, including your password for your domain registration. Then you're stuck with both no domain name and no money to show for it. Once again, you're safer to stick with doing everything through Escrow. com where the transaction can be verified and secure on both sides.

If you decide to accept bitcoin, intellectual property attorney Stevan Lieberman has an escrow service that accepts bitcoin at Escrow.domains. This would literally be the only way I'd accept bitcoin for a domain transaction.

Another corporate best practice is tagging certain domain names as "Not For Sale." One time I reached out to a company about a domain name they owned but were not actively using to see if they were open to an offer. Their response back was a wise one—they wouldn't be selling the domain for at least ten years because of the number of items in their systems tied to the old domain.

Their company had acquired this domain when buying another company and the IT department had warned decision makers that there were simply too many legacy systems with sensitive data attached to the domain name. The amount of time and money it would take to untangle these systems from the domain would not have only been costly—but disruptive to the business itself.

For example, before they exploded during the pandemic, Zoom's original domain was Zoom.us, not the top-tier Zoom.com they now have. But their systems for video calls, messaging, scheduling—basically the entire business infrastructure—were tied to Zoom.us.

So as of 2024, if you pay close attention to the meeting link for your next Zoom call, you might notice there is a "Zoom.us" still tucked away inside the link! Untangling their systems and data from the old domain would likely be catastrophic. And there's really no need for them to get rid of Zoom.us since it still aligns with their brand and they wouldn't want a bad actor to take it.

In these situations, there may be nothing anyone can do to move the needle on the decision—unless the price is right. If a potential buyer comes with the right amount that makes the time and work worth it, then perhaps the decision will get kicked up to the C-suite for consideration.

Another consideration you need to make is that of branding associated with a domain name not being actively used. This means intentional interdepartmental communication. So let's say the COO is looking over assets and sees the company has an unused domain name that could be worth in the millions—it's tempting to say, "Why hold onto this? Let's get it off the books and boost the bottom line!"

But just because a domain isn't being used now doesn't mean the company won't make use of it later on. Think about the iconic Volkswagen Beetle. It originally sold from 1950 to 1979 and was then discontinued. The Beetle was then resurrected to great popularity, starting in 1998 until 2011, and then the most recent generation ran from 2012 to 2019 before being discontinued again.

Does this mean Volkswagen is done with the name "Beetle"? Probably not. We shouldn't be surprised to see it one day resurrect, possibly as an EV model. It's still a part of the Volkswagen brand. Volkswagen appears to still own Beetle.com on the last check—and they'd be silly to part ways with it, even if it could net them a huge payday. (Although typing in Beetle.com currently doesn't even redirect to VW.com at this time. What a shame.)

When companies run into a situation like this, it might be the CMO who speaks up and says, "We still have an active brand trademark and we need to hold onto it." At any point, your legal, brand (marketing), or IT people need to have a voice and be able to veto the sale in order to protect the company's security—whether cyber, legal, or brand security.

TECHNICAL CHECKLIST

Given the high-risk aspect of transferring a domain name, companies should make sure they have a defined checklist to ensure safety. While this gets more into the technical/IT aspect of everything, it's essential you have a clear process for the transition.

You need to identify any dependencies attached to the domain, assess any firewall threat protections that could be an issue, or any ACH connections between the domain and the server. You need to examine whether an IRS account was ever associated with the domain name.

If your company does not yet have a checklist of technical items to address during a domain name transfer, consider using the following as a starting point. We used this for a recent transaction and while the seller's IT department modified it for their specific use, the feedback we got was that this was extremely helpful to them.

DOMAIN TRANSFER TECHNICAL NOTES[57]

1. Consider purchasing wildcard certificate.
2. Identify all third-party URL dependencies and strategy for conversion:

   a. Firewall & Threat protection vendors
   b. IRS transactions
   c. ACH transactions
   d. KnowBe4 Security Awareness Training
   e. Other

3. Copy existing site to new new branded site and fix all links.
4. Establish new XML sitemaps.
5. Add a structured data script for Organization to help Google identify the new domain as still being part of the main website.
6. Change http/https links to point directly to the new site.
7. Verify that the new site works.
8. Develop marketing campaign(s) of new branding to customers and other stakeholders.
9. Alter all internal apps' URLs to point to the new site.
10. Perform 301 redirects from old URL to new URL. Note: Don't forget .html, .pdf, .doc, etc. items.

Account for 10+ business days for the above full-time marketing items only.

1. Find links pointing to the site and contact endpoints to change URL. Note: This can be thousands of links.
2. Add/Change GSuite email domain and make new domain the primary (if you use GSuite, that is).

   a. TXT records, DKIM, SPF, DMARC changes for new site.
   b. Domain keys for CRM and other third-party tools.
   c. Advanced Gmail rules changes.
   d. Update all AD (Active Directory) accounts.
   e. App SMTP email changes.

3. Intranet site URL changes
4. Monitor redirects and sitemaps for at least 60-90 days. The longer the better for SEO optimization.
5. Deliver to Brannans (or your broker of choice) a list of all emails that need to be forwarded and specify the duration for forwarding. Note: Names are generally alright but forwarding for role-based emails like Admin@CompanyName.com or Finance@CompanyName.com is not possible.

Additional Notes:

1. Run a local copy of anything associated with the old domain. This could include the current public-facing website, intranet, landing pages, marketing pages, etc.
2. Have local computer hostnames adjusted to access the website as it currently stands. There will be issues if mass find/replace is attempted on databases to a new URL. Having access to "how it was" is essential.
3. Swap GSuite/Google Workspace URL before the old domain is transferred. This could cause loss of data if the new owner tries to add it to GSuite before it has been released by the original owner.[58]

You'll want to have a comprehensive meeting with your own team to go over this list and add any specific actions for your company. The more systems you have in place, the more you will want to check for any potential crossover with the domain name *before* it is transferred to the buyer.

If at any point you discover a sticking point or a new hurdle, then the key will be to communicate this to all the stakeholders, including the buyer. Discuss the situation and whether it will demand any changes in the proposed timeline for the transfer. Keeping an open line of communication will reinforce the trust already established during the negotiation and keep the deal moving forward even with additional hurdles.

Yet again, this is where a domain broker is an added asset to the process. While we can't advise on the specific technical processes, we can be instrumental in the communication and keeping everyone happy until the final deal is done.

SOME FINAL SECURITY THOUGHTS

In the digital domain, we can't ignore cybersecurity risks—whether you're an individual or a corporation. But as the old saying does, "The bigger they are, the harder they fall." When the issue of selling a domain name is brought up to your company, it should immediately trigger you to get input from multiple stakeholders. We're happy to give you free, confidential advice if you'd like to discuss this with us as well. (Of course, we're happy to sign an mNDA if necessary.)

Those of us who have been in the industry for decades have been a part of so many corporate transactions, we can advise you on the pitfalls, best practices, and if nothing else, be an additional soundboard while making your decision.

As in so many parts of life, a healthy dose of skepticism and caution can help you sidestep risks. But always remain curious in your caution so you don't miss a great opportunity.

As arduous as it may be, companies may find the act of untangling an old domain name helps them eliminate inefficiencies they've been dealing with for years. Beyond the financial benefit of the sale itself, it can help them innovate and streamline their business. Or they may find that holding onto so many unused domain names is itself a security risk and selling them off would actually make the company *more* secure from bad actors. After all, the more "swampy" your systems are, the more likely a cybercriminal can exploit a vulnerability and steal from you.

So if you're reading this and you've been tasked with researching how to handle the old domain names your company has acquired, the best place to start is with a conversation. Let's connect and see what makes sense for the security of the company—not only for now, but for the long-term.

SECTION V
CASE STUDIES

CHAPTER 21

BRANDING EXAMPLES

BEFORE DIVING INTO the promised stories of this chapter, we need to set some expectations. If you've read up to this point chronologically, then you will have already learned much of what can be taught about domain names—at least, what can be taught in book form. That said, Section V will give you the chance to see how everything we've discussed comes together with practical examples of real-life domain name acquisitions.

But let's say you've flipped here because you love a good case study. That's alright, too. You can consider this entire section the TL;DR of the book—or the "crash course" if you will. This section of the book is different from the other sections because it will be less information-driven and more story-driven.

This particular chapter is going to share a few broad, general case studies related to branding which will illustrate multiple principles discussed throughout the book. The following chapters for the remainder of the section will be more rapid-fire, short case study examples of specific topics and concepts.

Some of these have been referenced in earlier chapters but you'll also find new examples and stories I haven't used yet. One of the great parts of being a broker for so long is there's definitely no shortage of stories to tell in our industry!

By the time you finish this section, you'll not only have a better understanding of how the industry works, but you'll likely be asking what part of the story you are going to play. Launch a startup with a killer domain name for your brand? Upgrade your current domain name to a more premium name so you can get the ROI? Sell the premium domain name you've had for twenty-plus years?

Wherever you eventually land, there's a story here for you. So with that out of the way, let's get into some of my personal favorite case studies throughout my career.

WEB TRAFFIC (CHEESECAKE.COM)

When I first started in the domain name industry, it was with the perspective of an investor. When a friend—and later colleague—told me how much he had made from "flipping" domain names like some people flip houses, I couldn't believe it. Soon, I was seeing ".COM" behind every single item behind me—and then started my own portfolio of domain names.

Before I started Brannans as a full-fledged broker, I went to a domain auction in Milan, Italy where a pretty interesting—and tasty—domain was being sold: Cheesecake.com.

The name was being offered up by an investor who was using a small "mom and pop" bakery to make and ship cheesecakes nationwide. Long story short, I did some "back of the napkin" math and figured sales could be increased 10x within three to six months with the right SEO.

I ended up winning the auction and brought on a friend, Harvey Kaplan, as a business partner. Within three months, our sales had increased so much, we had to look for a supplier that could keep up with the increased volume of orders. We ranked number one for the term "cheesecake" on Google for a few years, too.

I learned a valuable business lesson: If you have a premium domain name, be ready for scaling to happen. We grew so quickly we had to scramble to meet demand to maintain our growing brand and reputation.

In Cheesecake.com—I saw an investment opportunity. I figured that if I built a business there that it was only a matter of time until interested buyers came knocking—and they did. At one point, I was hearing from a number of interesting prospects, including a well-known flower delivery service.

So who did I end up selling to? Eventually, I struck a deal with Ryan Abood. His mother Trudy had started a small flower shop in Massachusetts, but he wanted to help her expand the company's reach, specifically through the internet. He noticed that some of the best-selling items in the shop were gift baskets and had the idea to shift the business in a new direction.

He helped her set up Gourmet Gift Baskets—and put in the work to live up to the "gourmet" part of their name. He was so great at this, he caught the attention of a TV personality you might have heard of—Oprah Winfrey—and ended up on her show to talk about their gift baskets.

Even with this great publicity, he knew success is about more the long-term. Being featured on *Oprah* is great, but attention spans are short these days—and people will forget about you by the time the next episode airs. He knew one key to scaling their traffic and business was in acquiring desirable, keyword domain names.

In addition to GourmetGiftBaskets.com, Ryan also now owns Cheesecake.com, Strawberries.com, and GiftBaskets.com.

THE ALTERNATIVE TLD DEBACLE (O.CO)

Few things in this world irk me more than alternative TLDs—that is, the alternatives to .COM like .CO and .XYZ. What the brief history of domain names has taught us is that .COM is the most valuable TLD to have for your domain name—and you can actually hurt your company by going with one of the alternatives.

It's difficult—if not impossible—to control human behavior. And people are so conditioned to typing in ".COM" behind a domain name that you could end up losing money and traffic by going with the alternative. Which is exactly what happened with Overstock.

In many ways, Overstock helped give birth to e-commerce when they launched in 1999. Ten years later, they were doing a billion dollars in revenue and had become a household name.

Until 2009, the TLD .CO could only be used for entities in the country of Colombia since it is their ccTLD (country code TLD) the same way that .CA is the ccTLD for Canada. But in mid-2009, the board of ICANN[59] approved for .CO to be re-delegated so anyone could use it.

In 2011, Overstock decided it was time for a rebrand—that perhaps they could boost their SEO and sales traffic with a shorter name. Since "O.com" was not available for use, they needed to look into some other options.

I was a bit closer to the situation than others because I was speaking to Overstock's founder, Patrick Byrne, about a very short, alternative domain name so they could have the shorter name but still have the power of the .COM working in their favor. It didn't work out, though, and they decided to go with the alternative of "O.co." Because it was even shorter, they assumed this would be more desirable for consumers.

Well, it wasn't.

Despite the millions they had spent on advertising that "Overstock.com is now O.co," consumers kept typing in "O.com," which took them absolutely nowhere, leading to frustration. It quickly proved to be a problem for the brand as they lost 61 percent of their traffic—not the boost they had hoped for. They were forced to course-correct, and returned to Overstock.com.

The debacle underscores two important lessons in the world of domain names:

1. Always go with the .COM, not the alternative TLD.
2. You can spend millions on a marketing campaign, but you can't change public perception.

When public perception and human behavior are against your plan, then it's time to change the plan. Otherwise, you're throwing money in the toilet. No amount of money was ever going to train people to type in ".CO" instead of ".COM." Instead, they created confusion for consumers which might just be the cardinal sin of marketing.

Their case study also proves that your name matters with web traffic, even when you're a household name. You never want to make a move that is going to turn type-in traffic *against* you—and alternative TLDs are a surefire way to make that happen.

STANDING OUT (RED.COM)

Brand power and names go hand-in-hand. So if you're looking to enter into an established market, going up against well-established brands, your only shot for success is to find a way to stand out.

Warren Buffett once made this point about the soft drink market by saying, "If you gave me $100 billion and said take away the soft drink leadership of Coca-Cola in the world, I'd give it back to you and say it can't be done."

So what do you do if you are a startup going into an established market? How do you stand a chance at competing?

Answer: Have an unforgettable name.

Your domain name is one of the greatest opportunities you have to be unforgettable. And the perfect case study of this concept is the digital camera company RED.

While it hasn't been disclosed how much the company spent to acquire the domain name Red.com, it was probably a pretty penny. After all, the name was originally registered way back in 1992 and RED Digital Cinema didn't exist until 2005. But no doubt Jim Jannard and the other co-founders of RED were playing the long game and acquiring the one-word, exact brand match was a no-brainer.

As you can imagine, cameras and film are a difficult market to enter. It's similar to breaking into the shoe industry or any other well-established sector. If you're going to even have a shot at success, you've got to have a way to stand out—and a name is the perfect way to do so.

RED's entire mission was to bring digital filming into the mainstream in Hollywood. In a century-old business like cinema, trying to go head-to-head with other camera companies was likely to backfire. Digital film was still a new concept—and not one being embraced by many mainstream directors and cinematographers at the time.

"RED" doesn't tell you what the camera company does, of course, nor is it a clever acronym. And it tells you absolutely nothing about the quality of their cameras. But it's easy to spell and easy to remember. And it doesn't hurt that it has an association with Hollywood when you think about "the *red* carpet."

A major breakthrough for the company was when Oscar-winning director Peter Jackson used a prototype Red One camera when making a short film *Crossing the Line*. Fellow Oscar winner Steven Soderbergh saw the results and decided to use a Red One camera on his movie *Che*. With such two powerhouses advocating for their products, a domino effect took place with other high-profile directors like Ron Howard and Lars von Trier jumping on the RED digital bandwagon.[60]

Eventually, the company has grown in popularity and in April 2024, they were acquired by Japanese camera company Nikon for a reported $85 million so that they can expand into the digital cinema market.

You can have the greatest product or service in the world—but that may not be enough on its own. A great name—accompanied by a premium domain name to drive traffic your way—can make you stand out above the noise and literally revolutionize an established industry.

BRAND EXPANSION (SCAN.COM)

When you're a startup, it's rare for you to be flush with cash in the beginning. You've first got to prove your concept and develop an MVP (Minimum Viable Product) if you're going to attract the attention—and funding—from investors.

That's exactly the situation a UK-based startup found themselves in back in 2017. They were working to address a common problem in the British healthcare system: Make it easier for patients to find and schedule MRIs.

In the beginning, they had to be mean and lean. They wanted to make sure they had "MRI" in their name, so they found "NationalMRIScan. com" available on GoDaddy. When I sat down with company co-founder Charlie Bullock, he recalled the decision, saying, "[It] was the cheapest domain name out there. It was probably under $10 . . . We just needed literally a domain name to host [the website] on."

After five years working solely in the UK, they gained traction and discovered they were onto something bigger. They heard that the American healthcare market faced the same challenges they were already solving for patients and physicians in the UK, but how would they expand into such a competitive marketplace as the US?

For starters, the "National" in their name was a problem. They were now seeking to go *Inter*national. But their original domain name had other problems:

- It wasn't a one-word name.
- It wasn't easy-to-remember.
- It limited them to MRI scans.

If they were to expand into the US, they would need to acquire a much better domain name and rebrand around it.

"We wanted something super-memorable because we understood that we're in a competitive space," Charlie recalled. "When you're trying to get healthcare professionals to remember you, there's a thousand other companies competing for their time and attention. Same with patients and consumers . . . so we were looking for a name which, once you told someone the name, they wouldn't have to try very hard or write it down on a piece of paper to remember it."

They landed on Scan.com and then they reached out to me to help them get the domain name. The only major obstacle was that the domain name was owned by a VC group and the asking price was 10x more than they had in the bank at the time.

Together, we worked on opening the conversation with the owner to see what kind of arrangement he was open to. Thankfully, he was willing to consider an owner-financed arrangement. We could use Escrow.com's holding transaction capabilities to allow their startup to use Scan.com as they paid it off. Escrow would honor the payment arrangement we had negotiated and make sure the payments made it back to the seller. In the event of default, the registration would revert back to the seller who would then be able to sell it again if he wanted.

Everyone was happy with the arrangement—so we moved forward.

NationalMRIScan.com became Scan.com and now they had a real shot at building a successful, international brand.

Within two years of switching to Scan.com, the company raised $65 million from investors.

During our conversation, Charlie noted how this has been a major win for them. "Direct traffic now accounts for a decent percentage of our overall mix," he said.

This is key when you think about the cost of acquisition for new customers. If you do some calculations, a great domain name which naturally attracts traffic ends up saving you a ton of money because you avoid the need for monthly ad spend to stay ahead of your competitors. Even if you spend seven figures on a premium domain name, you may actually be saving yourself millions later on in ad spend. That's the power of a one-word .COM!

But this wasn't the only benefit that excited him.

"There's word of mouth," he explained. "Your [physician] tells you to go to Scan.com to get yourself an MRI scan . . . it's the memorability factor."

This was exactly what they had hoped for when they had rebranded—a memorable, easy-to-spell name that would help their company grow through word-of-mouth. If it's easier for physicians to remember, they'll mention it to patients more often. And if it's easy for patients to remember, the more likely they will end up on the site.

Your brand name is not only functional—it's your greatest lead magnet. Expanding your market share isn't always about outreach, it's also about drawing more people to you.

REINVENTING YOUR BRAND TO SUCCESS (RING.COM)

Sometimes a name change is more than just swapping out one label for another. Sometimes it's an entire reinvention of a brand's personality and purpose. That was the case with Ring, started by Jamie Siminoff.

Like so many other tech giants before him, Jamie had started the company out of his garage and called it Doorbot, including acquiring the domain name. The initial idea behind the company was to give people an easy way they could use their phone to see if a package had arrived—or to tell a solicitor to go away without having to actually answer the door. The sales pitch was built around the idea of convenience.

When the company launched in 2013, it was completely crowdfunded, but then Jamie found himself with an opportunity to go onto Shark Tank to pitch Doorbot. "I was broke when I went on Shark Tank," he once said. Everything seemed to be riding on it.[61]

Unfortunately, he didn't get the backing he was hoping for. But not all was lost.

In the process of pitching his idea, Jamie realized the convenience angle didn't have enough emotional impact. What actually seemed to grab people wasn't the convenience factor—but the security benefit of a doorbell camera. Especially as early users reported stories of police using video footage to help catch would-be burglars.

This necessitated an entire identity shift for the company—one built around safety. "Doorbot" was unable to communicate this reinvention of the brand. Soon, his sights were set on the name *Ring*.

As you can imagine, a name like Ring.com could appeal to multiple markets—especially the jewelry business, wedding industry, or even a family-run business like "Ring Movers" or "Ring Construction."

Jamie got Ring.com for $1 million in 2014. At the time, he only had $187,000 in the bank. To close the deal, he offered to pay the owner $187,000 down with the remaining $813,000 to be paid over two years.

Not only did the deal allow Ring to acquire the best name for their rebrand, but they could start reaping the benefits of a premium domain name's web traffic to drive sales. Also, no doubt the pressure of making the payments on Ring.com likely lit a fire under him and the team to succeed!

In 2018, it all paid off when Amazon bought Ring for an estimated $1 billion. Even though the purchase of the premium domain name was $1 million, it was worth the price!

And in 2023, Ring.com's annual gross sales were $1.097 billion!

Of course, Ring isn't the only company to make an identity shift for success—but it's impressive because of the direct relation of the premium domain name to their eventual success. Jamie may have been rejected in the *Shark Tank*, but without that "setback," it's possible the identity shift to Ring may have never happened.

BOOSTING CONVERSION RATE (FRIDA.COM)

But what if you don't need to reinvent your brand's identity or mission? Does upgrading a name still make a difference?

The answer is a resounding YES.

Having a one-word .COM has one of the most interesting benefits when it comes to the human psyche—it creates trust. When someone sees a one-word .COM, they automatically associate in their mind that you are the go-to for your industry. With that trust, you can count on conversions to go up. And what's really interesting is how this holds true even if your domain name doesn't specifically relate to what you do.

Take FridaBaby, the baby products company. They've created some of the most innovative baby products on the market. Maybe you've heard of the NoseFrida – the snot-sucker that lets parents gently and effectively clear their baby's stuffy nose. A hygienic filter ensures no snot ever reaches the parent's mouth, even though the idea might seem a bit unconventional. But guess what? It's super effective!

The problem for Frida is that when they were expanding, the domain name Frida.com wasn't available, so they had to go with the less-optimal FridaBaby.com. They were still registering decent sales and growing, but they also knew they had an issue with getting people onto their site. People kept typing "Frida.com" instead of "FridaBaby.com," which meant additional ad spend to make sure potential customers were getting routed the right way.

Meanwhile, the owner of Frida.com was a lady in Norway who had been using the name for her personal email ever since the '90s. And for years, she had been telling anyone that asked that her domain name wasn't for sale.

With a little bit of back-and-forth correspondence, though, we were able to establish trust and to get her thinking about a price. Despite the years of saying "No," it only took a few months for us to negotiate the sale—and everyone walked away happy.

Frida's mission and purpose stayed the same—creating great baby products for parents. Only their domain name was changing. But as soon as they made the move from FridaBaby.com to Frida.com, they saw an impact on their sales numbers. Bounce rates went down, traffic went up, and conversions went up. They didn't need to spend as much on ads to make sure people could find them, which further helped offset the cost of acquiring the domain name.

While moving to a one-word .COM isn't going to be an option for every brand, it can prove to be the single most profitable investment you make. So if you want your bounce rate to go down and your conversations to go up, moving to a one-word .COM just may be the ticket.

CYBERSECURITY & BRAND PROTECTION (GOOGLE.COM)

What if you had the opportunity to buy Google.com for only $12? Well, that's exactly what happened with former Google employee Sanmay Ved in 2015.

Now, it's important to note that Mr. Ved had no ill intentions towards the company who ended up rewarding him. Why? Because he uncovered a major security flaw which could have inflicted great damage on their brand.

He was on Google Domains one day when he noticed, to his surprise, that Google.com was available for purchase—at only $12. He clicked "buy" and—even more to his surprise—the transaction went through. He was the proud new owner of one of the most desirable domains you could imagine.

At least, for one minute. Because he had used Google Domains for the purchase, their system flagged the transaction and the company was able to take ownership back and refund his $12 purchase. Mr. Ved then reached out to the security team to let them know what happened—and they gave him $6,006.13 (which spells Google numerically) as a "bug bounty." And because Mr. Ved is a saint, when Google heard he was going to give all the money to a charity, they doubled the amount.[62]

Now imagine what would have happened if a bad actor had acquired the domain name from the security flaw. Maybe the tech giant would have caught it in time like they did with Mr. Ved, but maybe not. It's entirely possible a bad actor could have quickly transferred the name to another registrar and held it hostage—or done something even more nefarious which would have affected literally *billions* of people using Google.

While this particular case study can be seen as a wild outlier, it underpins an important issue—if Google can have security breaches, then so can *you*. Your domain name is one of the most valuable assets you have, no matter what you paid to acquire it. So spend the time and resources necessary to make sure it is secure.

Many domain name management companies (like CSC) offer renewal protection so that you can make sure your registration is automatically renewed each year. This is such a simple step to ensuring you hold onto it, and many of these companies also have tools and resources to help you retrieve a domain name in the rare event someone is able to steal it away.

CONCLUSION

The stories here have focused squarely on the relationship between domain names and your brand—and the power they wield for branding. Even if you're not in the market to buy but to sell, these are key principles to understand. Because when you recognize the potential brand power in the domain name you hold, then you can leverage it towards the right buyer. And not only will the right buyer be willing to pay you a premium price for it, they'll be glad to!

In the next chapter, we'll focus more on short examples of how companies have strategically used domain names. But it's also good to see some examples of what not to do so you can avoid making a mistake which could hurt your brand.

CHAPTER 22

UPGRADING EXAMPLES

IT'S COMMON FOR startups to begin with a less-than-desirable domain name simply because they are strapped for cash. However, there's no rule that says you have to stay with that domain name forever, just like there's no rule that says your starter home has to be your forever home.

So if you find your brand in a situation where you're stuck with a second-rate domain name—it's alright. Many others have been there before you but have managed to escape it by acquiring the top-tier domain name of their dreams.

Granted, the better the name you can start out with, the better for your brand. But in this chapter, I want to encourage you with some examples of brands who have upgraded their names over time. You've already read some in the previous chapter, but it's helpful to see just how common this trend is. It's not too late to upgrade to the domain name of your dreams. And if you're struggling with ideas of what that could look like, perhaps the examples here will help get some creative juices flowing.

While this chapter's case studies will be more "rapid-fire," the real takeaway here is to see just how frequently upgrading happens—and the benefits it provides. Some of the brands you see here will be very familiar—others may be new to you but represent the principles and best practices we see in the industry.

As a quick aside, I should note that the use of these examples shouldn't be construed as any kind of endorsement for these companies—they are simply case studies for us to learn from. And despite the vast differences in brands and domains you'll see here, you should start to notice a clear trend: The brand who upgrade their domain name don't only have a better name—they get better results.

EXACT MATCH

Before Google updated their search engine in 2012, a popular SEO domain name "hack" employed by many companies was to use a keyword term as the SLD. This practice was abused by people who were driving traffic to spammy, ad-packed solitary webpages, so Google had to take action for the sake of their own brand.

Since then, the best policy for a domain name is a simple one—get the EMD (Exact Match Domain) for your brand. But this also applies to the idea of "owning" a term within your industry, such as the Lawn.com case study from the previous chapter. So let's look at a few other brands who have acquired exact match names in some creative ways to better position themselves for SEO.

GOLD.COM

The acquisition of Gold.com by JM Bullion in March of 2024 is a perfect example of a brand employing EMD. JM Bullion is a major e-commerce retailer for precious metals and had already acquired Silver.com in the past.

Gold.com has had a storied history. In 2019, Kay Jewelers sold it to an undisclosed Chinese firm[63]—who held onto it for five years before JM Bullion acquired it for a reported $8.5 million.[64] With both "gold" and "silver" under their belt, they've given themselves an impressive profile boost in terms of web ranking. Now, whenever someone types in "Gold. com," it leads them straight to JM bullion's site, which will undoubtedly be huge for their conversion rate.

VODKA.COM

Similarly, you've got the case of Russian Standard Vodka, owned by Russian billionaire Roustam Tariko. Way back in 2007, he had the foresight to leverage an EMD for his brand, which was already Russia's largest vodka maker.

At that time, he paid a reported $3 million to acquire vodka.com, just so it would redirect people to their website.[65] This would position the brand for international presence with the continued globalization brought on by the internet. And I have a feeling they won't be relinquishing the name any time soon.

TWITTER.COM (AND X.COM)

Twitter is an especially interesting case because their domain name tells a story of how the company shifted strategy. When it was first launched in 2006, founders Jack Dorsey and Ev Williams were focused on developing an "SMS-based texting service,"[66] not the social media giant it would become. As such, given the popularity at the time of text-based tools cutting out vowels, they acquired Twttr.com as their domain.

But once they decided to refocus the service on the web itself and its potential as a platform in the burgeoning space of social media, they decided they needed the vowels—and bought Twitter.com for the incredible deal of $7,500.

By 2010, the company was worth $1 billion and then in 2022, Elon Musk acquired the platform to the tune of $44 billion and quickly pushed a rebrand agenda to change it to X. A further twist in the plot is that Musk had already re-acquired "X.com" from PayPal in 2017—a domain he had sold to them three years earlier for $6.8 million. In a tweet published at the time, he said, "Thanks PayPal for allowing me to buy back X.com! No plans right now, but it has great sentimental value to me."[67]

While many criticized the move at the time, Musk is no fool when it comes to branding. And at the time of writing this chapter, his "sentimentality" appears to be paying as X is seeing an uptick in usage, proving once again that it pays to have the exact match .COM domain.

TWO-WORD SLD TO ONE-WORD UPGRADES

Two-word SLD domain names are sometimes inevitable. At times, they can even be an intentional choice for alignment with the brand.

A company like Best Buy comes to mind here. Since that is the proper name for the company, it makes more sense for them to have a two-word domain because it also aligns with customer behavior—people will type in "Best Buy near me" into Google, not "Best" or "Buy" by themselves. And they certainly won't be typing in "BB" as an abbreviation, though

Best Buy could have chosen to go that route with the domain name if they had wanted.

But typically, having a one-word SLD is better than two words. One famous example is how Facebook used to be TheFacebook.com—and once people started abbreviating the site as "FB" on a regular basis, it became a matter of brand protection for them to also acquire FB.com.

But let's look at some other brands who chose to drop the two-word SLD so they could scale their company through the power of a one-word domain name.

DRIP.COM

Drip, founded by Rob Walling who I met at a conference in 2016, is an email marketing company that has since been acquired by LeadPages. In the beginning, they had to be content with the domain name GetDrip.com. Even though they were experiencing steady growth, they needed to supercharge it—especially as more brands started to use drip email campaigns.

Once they had the cash to do so, it made sense for them to shift to the premium domain name Drip.com. Not only was it the exact match for their brand, but it's more memorable than "Get Drip," helping to boost their SEO and drive more traffic. It's likely this was a key move which eventually led to their sale to LeadPages.

ICE.COM

Ice.com is one of those domain names which has a storied history. It was once held by the online jewelry retailer Ice who had also acquired Diamond.com as part of their buyout of competitor Odimo. Of the total $9.5 million transaction for the Odimo buyout, $2 million was for the jewelry inventory—and the remaining $7.5 million represented the value of the domain names alone. Think about that for a second!

Still, there were plenty of brands keeping their eye on "Ice.com," especially when an Austin-based company bought Ice for $3 million in 2014. But when the company began to flounder, the question was who would get the premium name next?[68]

One of those companies who was watching and waiting for the opportunity was ICE (Intercontinental Exchange), which conducts financial exchanges and clearing house trades on a global scale—including operating the New York Stock Exchange even though they are headquartered in Atlanta, Georgia.

Founded in 2000, they were a $40 billion company—and yet the best domain they could have was TheIce.com. As you can imagine, this wasn't the best for their web traffic or search ability. But plenty of other companies were interested in the name too—obviously, some of those in the literal ice industry, food and beverage industry, and even in the jewelry sector since "ice" is a nickname for diamonds.

When Ice's new owners were closing shop, they discovered their domain names were literally their most valuable asset—so they decided to take Ice.com to auction. With such fierce competition, it became one of ICE's highest priorities to make sure they won the day—and they did. Today, they continue to reap the benefits of making the move from two words to one word.

TESLA.COM

We all think of Tesla today as a giant and the current undisputed champion of 100 percent electric cars, but it wasn't always so. When Elon Musk used his PayPal exit to found Tesla Motors, that's exactly the domain name they started with—TeslaMotors.com.

Tesla is an interesting case study because there's a legal component to it. The previous owner of Tesla.com was Stu Grossman who had owned it for years. A different company—Tesla Industries, Inc.—tried to sue him for the name, claiming trademark priority. Grossman fought back—and won.

So when it came time for Mr. Musk to pursue the name, he didn't make the same mistake as Tesla Industries. Instead, he played nice and found out what it was worth to Mr. Grossman. In 2018, Tesla Motors acquired the one-word domain name Tesla.com for $11 million.

As one article pointed out, "Dropping 'Motors' from Tesla's domain name cost $11 million, but it gave the company the freedom to advance with its plans to branch out."[69]

By becoming "Tesla," they could grow beyond cars into solar panels, solar storage batteries, solar roof tiles, and even developing solar fuel stations. For Musk, it wasn't just about the vanity of the one-word domain and web traffic—it was about the very vision of the company moving forward and opening new opportunities.

DROPBOX.COM

A pioneer in online storage and file sharing, Dropbox's domain name change was about more than just an upgrade for web traffic. Originally, Dropbox was a product name for the startup Evenflow, launched in May 2007 by Drew Houston.

But they ended up in a trademark dispute with Proxy, Inc. which required them to use the domain name of GetDropbox.com which was hurting their traffic since so many users would type in "Dropbox.com," assuming they owned the exact match, one-word domain name. It wouldn't be until 2009 when they were able to acquire Dropbox.com which then allowed them to fully rebrand to Dropbox, dropping the name of Evenflow entirely.

As reporter Jason Kincaid noted in his article covering the change, "There's no doubt Dropbox has been losing out on plenty of traffic and customers" before the change. Initially, they set it up for Dropbox.com to redirect to GetDropbox.com, but over time, they moved their systems so that Dropbox.com became the primary address.[70]

UPGRADING YOUR TLD

The hill I'm willing to die on is that .COM is the only TLD a brand should consider, at least if they are doing business in the US or on an international scale. If you're doing business in Canada, then I would give the same advice with .CA, or in France with .FR. But no matter how many new TLDs we see emerge, .COM has proved to be the "top dog" in terms of brand trust, web traffic, and memorability.

I know it can be tempting to go with the cheaper TLDs like .CO and .XYZ, especially when your exact match isn't available. In fact, maybe you've already registered the alternative TLD domain name and are building your website on it, but I'd suggest you use a second word like "Get" or "The" in front of your brand before you use a cheaper TLD like .CO or .XYZ.

The best next move you can make is to start planning for how you can upgrade to .COM. It might necessitate a name change if the owner is steadfast against selling—or you might need to start saving up for the down payment you'll need to make on an owner-financed deal.

ZOOM.COM

In 2018, Zoom was still a novelty video call service, though steadily growing. In 2020, they became a household name. Though no one could have foreseen the pandemic coming, possibly the smartest move they made leading up to their IPO in 2019 was upgrading their primary domain name from Zoom.us to Zoom.com, reportedly to the tune of $2 million.[71]

Certainly, it was a smart strategic move since the alternative TLD of .US is not exactly ideal for web traffic. But part of why the case study is so interesting is because Zoom still owns their original domain name of Zoom.us.

You might think a brand would sell off or release an alternative TLD name, but in Zoom's case, it would be a major liability. Zoom's call systems are still tied to the Zoom.us domain name, so getting rid of it would be catastrophic to their operations—and highly disruptive for customers.

Perhaps one day they will move their systems to Zoom.com and transition away from .US. But doing so will take an immense amount of time and resources. Even if they did that, from a standpoint of brand protection, it makes sense for them to keep the .US name so that a bad actor doesn't acquire it, so don't ever expect to see Zoom.us available for sale.

LINKTREE.COM

Popular link building tool Linktree employed a really creative domain name "hack" when they first launched. Since they couldn't yet afford the exact match of Linktree.com, they went down an unconventional route. Since .EE is the ccTLD (country code Top Level Domain) for the small nation of Estonia but was available for global use, they registered the domain Linktr.ee.

While this still is not as good as using the TLD of .COM, it was a creative way to have an "exact" match when people searched the web for them. In fact, to this day, Linktr.ee is their primary domain, though they acquired Linktree.com as a traffic booster and for brand protection. Perhaps one day they'll make the same move as Dropbox and move their systems over to Linktree.com, but their strategy serves as an interesting template for other scrappy startups.

BOX.COM

Like Dropbox, Box, Inc. is a cloud-based platform focused on content management and collaboration. But like so many other lean startups, they were not able to acquire the premium domain name of Box.com and had to settle for Box.net.

Unlike Dropbox, though, they shifted early on to focusing more on corporate customers rather than individuals, and with some rising investor interest (including from Mark Cuban), they were able to scale. Inevitably, this meant acquiring Box.com to avoid customer confusion and to boost web traffic. Like others mentioned here, they still own Box.net for brand protection, though it now redirects to Box.com.

VIO.COM

Vio is an interesting case study because they check multiple boxes of upgrading a name since they were originally started as FindHotel.net. As an educated guess, it appears that in the beginning they chose the name "FindHotel" to try to leverage some keyword power from search engines. But without the TLD of .COM, I'm willing to bet they continued to miss out on the traffic they wanted.

In fact, as their own Medium article about the name change reveals much of their thinking:

"Back when we launched FindHotel in 2016, we were big on ideas yet small on resources ... With our success came the realisation [sic] that our name and visual identity needed to transform."[72]

So not only did they upgrade to being a .COM, they shifted from a two-word name to one-word, along with an entire rebrand. Sometimes a drastic move like this is completely necessary when reshaping the vision of your brand. It may cause some brand confusion in the beginning, but no doubt they are seeing better results simply by moving to both a better TLD and an easy-to-spell, easy-to-remember name.

OPTIMIZATION & PROTECTION

In our digitally driven world, optimizing your name is no longer optional. It's imperative. It's part of how you set yourself apart, leverage web traffic, and even protect your brand.

When Google needed to restructure in 2015, it necessitated the creation of Alphabet Inc, which is now their parent company—even though Google came first. As part of its creation, Alphabet even acquired the unusual domain name abcdefghijklmnopqrstuvwxyz.com. While it may seem like a publicity stunt, it was likely a more strategic move to protect the brand and optimize their web presence. It's the same reason they also own misspelled domain names like Googl.com and Gogle.com and even GoogleSucks.com.[73] All a matter of smart defensive strategy.

At times, optimization even necessitates an entire name change for a company—or giving life to a specific product or service by setting it apart. So let's look at a few ways companies have used domain names to optimize their web presence, specifically related to their name or product names.

AMAZON.COM

Earlier in the book, we talked about how Amazon wasn't always Amazon. When Jeff Bezos founded the company, he originally filed under the name of "Cadabra."

Unfortunately, the name Cadabra fails a couple of the tests for a good domain name. First, it's not easiest to spell. Some might think it starts with a "k" or through in an extra "d" or a "u." If a third-grader struggles to spell a word, then it's not the best domain name.

Second, it fails the "radio test." The reason Bezos decided to change was because several people thought he said "cadaver" instead. Forgive the pun, but he knew then the name was dead in the water.

As a generic term—Amazon—is a far better option, of course. Sharing a name with the second largest river in the world is a special bonus in terms of attracting web traffic, and it also didn't hurt that it starts with the letter "A."

Another "prime" example with Amazon is that of Amazon Prime. As the service grew into its own platform, it made sense for them to acquire Prime.com to replace the old URL, which was Amazon.com/prime. This would not only optimize the platform for search engines but help distinguish it as its own brand.

HOME.COM

Once upon a time, Homefinity Mortgage registered the domain name Homefinity.com. From an exact match standpoint, this makes sense. But the real question is whether it's the best name for driving traffic your way?

It's one thing if someone is searching for you specifically. For instance, anyone can find me if they go to Google and type in "David Clements domain name broker Brannans." But how many people will actually do that?

What you really want is for someone to type in a keyword for your industry—and *then* find you. So in my case, that would mean someone typing in "domain name broker" and finding me on the front page of Google.

So for Homefinity, they had to reevaluate whether the exact match name was actually the right fit for their marketing goals. Ultimately, they discovered they could get more traffic if they changed their domain name to the keyword people type the most often when they are exploring a mortgage—"home."

While the name of the company didn't change, the website did. They acquired the premium domain name of Home.com to boost their SEO and web traffic. As of this writing, Home.com redirects to Homefinity's parent company of Fairway Mortgage.

PAW.COM

For all of you dog people out there, Paw.com is an online retailer of high-quality pet products, with their marquee items being their dog beds.

But before they were Paw, they started out under the name Treat A Dog, including using the domain name TreatADog.com

You probably already see the problem, though. For starters, "Treat A Dog," while a cute name, is too many words for a truly optimized name. It doesn't match up with a common search phrase, and it also doesn't quite pass the memorability test.

No doubt the owners figured this out pretty quickly. And they knew the answer would mean entirely renaming the company—and acquiring the premium domain name Paw.com. But with its easy spelling and clear association with pets, it was definitely the right choice for branding, especially with driving traffic to their site and a higher conversion rate.

In his book *Start. Scale. Exit. Repeat.* Paw co-founder Colin Campbell even discusses the reasons for the domain name acquisition in terms of both optimization and protection:

> "In short, the name Paw.com created a moat for the business by giving us the opportunity to sell products under a specific, easily recognizable brand name that helped us build credibility and strengthen our relationship with our customers—something no competitor could take away from us."[74]

SHIELD.COM

As we've touched on before, cybersecurity is essential in the modern world. Fraud prevention company SHIELD is on a mission to identify bad actors and stop them from defrauding companies.

But when they first started out, the company was known as "Cash Shield" with the exact match domain name CashShield.com. Like some of the previous examples, though, this was certainly not the most optimized name.

First, it's a two-word domain instead of one-word. It's also not keyword friendly as it doesn't immediately relate to fraud protection. The name also doesn't pass the "radio test" because the "sh" in both "cash" and "shield" run together when you sound it out aloud, which could lead some people to think the name is "Cashield" instead. And from a business perspective, it's also a limiting name because the word "cash" makes it sound like they only protect physical currency, not digital transactions.

Switching to the name and exact match domain of Shield.com addresses all these problems. It's easier to spell, easier to remember, has a more obvious connection to protection from fraud, passes the "radio test," and provides a larger scope for services. And like some other examples, they still retain their original CashShield.com domain but it redirects to Shield.com, the more SEO-friendly name.

PINK.COM

No, we're not talking about the singer—we're talking about the PINK apparel line from Victoria's Secret. The line has been so successful for the company, it really has taken on a life of its own.

In 2007, Victoria's Secret purchased Pink.com for $1.5 million. Before the acquisition of the name, the brand had been using the less-ideal VSPink.com for the clothing line.

When it comes to protecting a valuable brand, companies will do whatever they need to.[75] As of the writing of this book, the domain redirects to PINK's dedicated page on the Victoria's Secret website, but it's likely the move was made both for optimization and brand protection.

ACRONYMS

Thirty years ago, all the marketing books I read offered the same advice: "Don't use acronyms." At least, that was the advice unless you were a huge company or had been around for a long time—like International Business Machines (IBM) and General Electric (GE).

However, that's not necessarily 100 percent true today. Some brands, including smaller brands, can move to acronym-based domains more quickly. And sometimes it can be more desirable, especially if you're able to get the .COM rather than having to settle for an alternative TLD. And in the event you already are a well-established brand, it can be an especially smart move for brand and trademark protection.

Case in point:

AMERICAN AIRLINES (AA.COM)

It takes a long time to type "AmericanAirlines.com," so it shouldn't be a real surprise that the US's largest airliner opts for the domain name AA.com. Not only is it shorter and a premium name, but it also aligns with their brand in terms of the logo design.

In fact, they were definitely keeping an eye on the digital horizon as they bought AA.com for $75,000 way back in 1997 to make the brand more compatible with the internet. It was an incredibly smart move, saving them potentially millions from having to acquire it later on like some brands who didn't take the internet as seriously.

THE NEW YORK TIMES (NYT.COM)

While the *New York Times*'s primary domain is NYTimes.com, they made the brand protection move to acquire NYT.com as well, which redirects to the main page. Since this is a common acronym used by the paper as shorthand, it also allows them to leverage SEO for uses of "NYT" by external sources.

ABBVIE (RA.COM)

With the pharmaceutical company AbbVie, we also see a similar approach to acronyms as what we saw with JM Bullion's acquisition of Gold.com. They bought RA.com since RA is a well-known abbreviation for rheumatoid arthritis, one of the specific health conditions they focus on treating.

This type of acronym acquisition is closely related to optimization. Since AbbVie knows people are more likely to search "RA" than "AbbVie," the acquisition makes good business sense. They've honed in on the problem—and want to funnel people towards them as the solution.

AMERICAN HOME SHIELD (AHS.COM)

Home warranty company American Home Shield is yet another example of when acronyms can be an asset to a brand. Once again, typing in American Home Shield takes more time, not to mention "shield" can be easily misspelled when typing quickly. By using the domain name

AHS.com, they are able to circumvent this customer hassle, while also having a premium three-letter domain name. After all, there are only 17,576 ways that you can combine three letters in the English alphabet.

Now, you might say, "David, that's great for those huge companies, but it doesn't sound practical for us." But regardless of your brand's size, this strategy of using acronyms (especially the AbbVie example) serves as an incredible marketing template to consider if you have an organization that overlaps with a well-known acronym.

For instance, let's say you are developing an organization devoted to addressing Post Traumatic Stress Syndrome for veterans. Even if you choose some other name for your company, it could make good branding sense to acquire a name like PTSD.com or PTSD.org. When figuring out what will best drive traffic to your site, you need to keep all the options open and test them to see what works best.

CONCLUSION

Our industry is full of story after story of how brands have upgraded their domain names for different reasons. Here's a few others you might want to dig into more:

- Acoustic—Upgraded from Acoustic.co to **Acoustic.com**
- Angel Studios—Acquired **Angel.com**
- Archer Aviation—Upgraded from FlyArcher.com to **Archer.com**
- Bird—Upgraded from MessageBird.com to **Bird.com**
- Bubble—Upgraded from Bubble.io to **Bubble.com**
- Clubhouse—Upgraded from JoinClubhouse.com to **Clubhouse.com**
- DC Comics—Upgraded from DCComics.com to **DC.com**
- Gravity Forms—Acquired **Gravity.com**
- HBO—Acquired **Max.com**
- Hubspot—Acquired **Connect.com**
- Synchrony—Upgraded from SynchronyFinancial.com to **Synchrony.com**
- Uber—Upgraded from UberCab.com to **Uber.com**

- Universal Pictures—Upgraded from UniversalPictures.com to **Universal.com**
- Woo Commerce—Rebranded to **Woo.com**

When you dig into the reasons for each of these upgrades and acquisitions, it's not just for a prettier name on a website. And it's not a vanity exercise. It's a solid strategic business move. So whether you are a founder ideating your startup's name or the marketing director at a Fortune 500, let these case studies serve as your food for thought on how you can best optimize and protect your brand.

And if you're reading this and have a premium domain name in your portfolio, pay even closer attention. Brands are willing to spend the money for that premium domain name. It's just a matter of deciding who you feel comfortable handing it off to and when. So in our final chapter of case studies, we'll get into a couple of examples of what the buying and selling process can look like.

CHAPTER 23

BUYING & SELLING EXAMPLES

A S A BROKER, customer confidence is not something I take lightly. Many of the deals I helped broker have very specific NDAs in place, which sometimes limit how much I can say about them. That's alright, though, because it's always better to have trust with a client than a cool story to tell.

That said, this section of the book wouldn't be complete without a couple more examples of the buying and selling process. So since I myself have a long history as a domain name buyer, I want to invite you behind the scenes of one of my favorite acquisitions ever—Batteries.com.

BATTERIES.COM

When Batteries.com first caught my eye, it was owned by Audiovox (now known as Voxx International). Back in the 1960s, Audiovox had made their mark in electronics with brands like Jensen speakers.

Over time, though, they moved away from public-facing products and more into the components side of electronics, including building some of the components in Apple products. As part of their diversification strategy, they had acquired Batteries.com for $20.5 million. Prior to the acquisition, Batteries.com had been a wholesale distributor for Energizer, putting their products into retail outlets like Best Buy.

For five years, I kept reaching out and asking if they'd be willing to sell me the name. The website was active and it had been online for sixteen years, but it looked like it hadn't been updated in a while. I didn't need the whole battery business—just the domain name. With each call, I would up my offer, wanting to prove to them I was serious. But time after time, I got the same answer, "No, it's not for sale at this time."

At the risk of burning them out, I finally said, "How about I just follow up with you in six months. Would that be alright?"

My contact there said that would be fine and I set a reminder in my email for exactly six months—and I moved on.

Fast forward five years—the reminder popped up for the twelfth time. This time when I reached out, I was told that they were considering selling Batteries.com. I got an email the following week from a new contact who hadn't been privy to the many other calls and emails I had made before.

"Give us a month to chat about this and we'll get back to you," he said.

It wasn't much hope—but at least it was a foot in the door. When we reconnected after a month, I was pleasantly surprised when he said, "Okay, we're open to selling," and then quoted a price that was actually $50K less than my current offer.

Well, this was an interesting turn of events. I've always loved a good negotiation, so I couldn't help myself and asked, "Is there any wiggle room?"

And then, right there on the phone, with hardly a second passing by, he dropped the price by another $50K and added, "But that's as low as we'll go. Otherwise, we'll just take it to auction."

At that point, I knew I'd done as much as I could and said, "No problem, I'll take it." By some miracle of circumstance, I had just saved $100,000 on a domain name held by a public company—simply because they had not recorded my previous offers.

The moral of the story here is that when it comes to buying, it's always best to let the seller set the price first. If you try to do it, you might offend them with a lowball offer and kill any chance of a deal. But if you let them set the price first—you might discover they undervalue the name, or at least figure out where you can negotiate.

And if you're a corporation selling a name, the moral is to keep track of your communications. I was willing to honor my previous offers—but they were the ones who offered to sell it for less.

When it came time to close the deal, I ended up getting even more than I bargained for and they agreed to not only sell me the name but the actual battery distribution company along with it. I figured why not and took possession batteries that were stored in two different warehouses. It was a bit of a hassle moving the batteries from New York down to Georgia, but for a few years, it was a good extra source of income until I decided to shut it down in 2019.

My acquisition of Batteries.com was a big deal at the time because of how much Audiovox had paid for it to begin with. But ultimately, the only real asset had been the Batteries.com name itself. The inventory, Chinese connections, and distribution deals were valuable but not as much as the domain name. In some ways, I had no business going after the name—except that I *made* it my business because I've always thought it was one of the most valuable domain names ever registered.

If there's another lesson to be learned here for buyers, it's the power of gumption and tenacity. It would have been easy to talk myself out of even approaching such a big company, to say, "No way would they ever sell this name to an individual." But guess what? That's exactly what they did. And they did so because I kept coming back and showed how serious I was.

It's this same kind of tenacious energy I put into any deal I'm working for a client, whether they are trying to buy a domain name from an individual or a corporation. Gumption and tenacity, hand-in-hand. You don't have to take the "No" and walk away. You can always ask to follow up. Company priorities change. And sometimes selling that domain name gives them the liquidity they want for other priorities. So whatever you do—*don't give up.*

Oh, and if anyone reading this is interested in buying Batteries.com, then give me a call.

SCAN.COM

I'm incredibly grateful for the clients who have given me permission to share their stories throughout the book—but especially to Charlie Bullock at Scan.com who I introduced back in Chapter 21. Thanks to Charlie's generosity, I get to go a bit deeper into his story here to show why this acquisition was such a big deal, both for him and the seller.

When NationalMRIScan.com was looking to upgrade their name so they could expand into the US and optimize their web traffic, Scan.com was a clear favorite. The name was available for sale—but it wasn't going to come cheap.

At the time, it was owned by Idealab, who describe themselves as "the longest running technology incubator" with an impressive 150-plus companies under their belt in their nearly thirty year history.[76] To put it bluntly—when it comes to domain name owners, you can't find anyone more savvy than they are.

Besides Scan.com, they own hundreds of other premium domain names in their portfolio. When I discovered this, I was frank with National MRI Scan, telling them, "Look, you're not going to be able to get much of discount from them. This is part of their very business, so you'll have to pay them what they think it's worth—or more."

But because I knew domain names were part of their business, that also meant we had an exciting possibility before us. "You know, they might be willing to consider doing an owner-financed deal. It's going to be a big investment, but it will be worth it."

Thankfully, the National MRI Scan team knew the potential available to them if they could acquire the name—so they gave me the green light. My instincts turned out to be right and the good people of Idealab were indeed open to a financing arrangement.

What we landed on was a manageable down payment, fair recurring payments that would allow National MRI Scan time to scale and adjust their budget, and a balloon payment at the end of the agreement. Everyone got to walk away happy.

Best of all is how the acquisition and name change has worked out for Scan.com. When they first approached me, they had only raised a pre-seed round. Since then, they've raised $65 million in capital investments, and I believe they're working on a large funding round as I write this—the name change has helped them make their way into the American market and attract new customers and partnerships. The way they are growing, by the time the funding round is closed, the acquisition cost for the domain name Scan.com will be a rounding error compared to their market cap.

Once again, we can find lessons here for both sellers and buyers. If you're selling a premium domain name, be open to the possibility of an owner-financed deal for the buyer. With Escrow.com's holding transactions, there is really nothing to lose. You end up making more on the deal than a straight cash buyout—and in the unlikely event of default, you get the domain name back and you can sell it again if you like.

The same goes for buyers—a finance deal can get you the premium domain name that's going to help your business scale right away and lights a fire under you. It's human nature to take better care of whatever we value the most.

WHO, NOT WHAT

Many times, I've found the key to a great transaction isn't about the name itself—it's about who is involved. If you're a buyer, knowing who the seller is and how they value the name is key to how you approach them. You always want to do so with great respect—never from a place of trying to guilt or bully them into giving up a name.

If you're a seller, knowing who is making the offer is the determining factor in how confident you can be in their offer. So if you're out to sell your domain name for the highest amount, the key is to sell to the people who have the most money and that they value domain names like the game-changing agents they are for a business.

For instance, let's say you're helping out with a fundraiser for a charitable cause you care about and you've committed to raising a certain dollar amount. Who are you going to call to pitch in? You're going to call people and businesses that you know have more discretionary income available to them for donations.

It's no different in the domain name space. It matters who you sell to. As a broker, whether I'm helping a seller or a buyer, that's a major part of my job. Finding out who is behind the name or behind the offer. It's about helping sellers find the best buyers—and helping buyers connect with sellers for the best deal.

Once we know the "who," we can figure out a strategy. We may be dealing with intangible, digital assets, but the business itself is still centered on people. People with stories, people with ambitions and dreams. We shouldn't let some dollar signs and a .COM make us lose sight of this truth.

CONCLUSION

We humans really like names. Not just our own—we love naming *everything*. Children give names to their dolls and stuffed animals. Adults give names to their cars and boats. Heck, we even name our WiFi routers just because we don't like seeing labels like ATT8ip620. Naming is in our DNA. We can't help ourselves!

Why?

Because names hold great power, value, and significance.

The best businesses know this. They know a name is also a form of communication. Your name communicates your story, your reputation, your identity. It's why some brands become indistinguishable from their function—Levi's, Hoover, Kleenex, Google. A great name is integrated fully with your purpose.

Remember, in the digital age, domain names are your storefront. They are the first contact point between you and a customer. It's your opportunity to be *known*—and often, it's your opportunity to be *found*.

You can't always put a dollar sign on that—as much as we may try to.

With nearly forty years of history, domain names are now part of the fabric of the modern economy. Understanding how they work is no longer for the "tech-savvy" out there—it's a matter of survival. A great domain name can end up being the most valuable asset you control.

You don't need me to tell you the world will keep changing. New markets will emerge. New tech will launch—and along with it, a host of new business opportunities. Don't overlook the importance of the domain name.

Let's recognize that you might still have questions. No worries. No book can be the "end all, be all" of information on any topic, much less one as complex as domain names. So don't see this as the end of the book, but rather as the start of your journey. No question is dumb or off-limits. Reach out and let's connect.

While I can't work with everyone out there, our team is always willing to at least get people moving in the right direction. Sometimes that means delivering news they don't want to hear, such as, "I'm sorry, but you don't actually have a premium domain name to sell." Or maybe it's "Sorry, the corporation who owns the name has a 'Do Not Sell' tag in place on it for the next ten years."

Even with this kind of "bad" news, you can still be moving in the right direction. The best domain names move you forward—towards the brand you want to build, the legacy you want to leave behind.

At the back of this book, you'll find some helpful links and additional resources to help you get started. You can also visit Brannans.com or to reach out to us for a consultation.

Names have power. Names can last. Over 175 years later, we're still telling the story of Samuel Brannan, after all. Even if you didn't know his name, you've heard the sage advice: "In a gold rush, sell shovels."

The new gold rush is already here. In the digital age, new opportunities abound—in mobile apps, SaaS, the cloud, and AI. New problems require new solutions—and your business idea could be the next great solution. Your domain name could be your greatest shovel. But only if you know how you're going to use it. Only if it's the right size for you.

Domain names are a form of alchemy. They take simple letters and symbols and transform ideas into gold. So let's grab a shovel together—and go find some gold.

ABOUT THE AUTHOR

While waiting to find out if he would be accepted into medical school, David was introduced to the world of domain names. His two decades of experience have seen him travel the globe as a key player in over 10,000 domain name transactions, negotiating deals in over twenty languages across more than seventy-five countries. In 2012, he founded Brannans.com, which has earned a reputation as a premium domain name brokerage, earning a top ten position with Escrow.com numerous times. As a broker, David has overseen six and seven-figure domain transactions, including with high-profile brands like Hewlett-Packard and Frida.

David received his bachelor's degree in Biotechnology from Kennesaw State University and has become a go-to voice for identifying premium domain names for brands, especially for startups looking to scale. When he's not serving clients with their domain name needs, David spends his time on the water, or under the water with SCUBA, has traveled extensively around the world, and lives in Alpharetta, Georgia with his wife and two daughters.

GLOSSARY

301 redirect: A signal for permanently redirecting from on URL address to another, including transferring search engine ranking power.
Chapter: 20

Alternative TLDs: Less desirable top-level domains, such as .CO, .MOBI, .BIZ, .XYZ, which generally have a spike in popularity when they first emerge on the market but struggle to remain relevant over the long term.
Chapter: 1, 9, 21, 22

Anchoring Effect: The cognitive bias that occurs when you see a sticker price on anything. For instance, when many people see the pricing sticker on a vehicle, their mind becomes anchored to the price.
Chapter: 8, 18

Anticybersquatting Consumer Protection Act (ACPA) suit: A specific class of lawsuit in the US established in 1999 in which an individual or company can directly sue a cybersquatter for infringing on their trademark or intellectual property.
Chapter: 14

Brand/branding: The collection of an organization's intellectual property combined with the public perception that forms the public and private identity of the organization. It includes what you are recognized, noticed, and known for, along with the message you want to convey.
Chapter: 7, 8, 9,

BrandBucket.com: Domain name marketplace designed to help founders identify and acquire great domain names.
Chapter: 9, 17

Brand Protection Agencies (BPAs): Companies that assist brands in brand protection services, including protecting digital assets from theft, protecting from trademark infringement or IP-related issues, and going after bad actors such as cybersquatters.
Chapter: 3, 10, 16

Brokers: Individuals or companies that assist with facilitating domain name sales between parties, including negotiation of deals between parties, and assisting in the registration transfer. In a sales situation, a broker helps identify potential buyers, marketing domain names for sales or auctions. An acquisition broker assists buyers in the acquisition process, identifying ideal domain names for a brand and negotiating the acquisition with the current registrant.
Chapter: 3, 12, 16

Buyers: Any individual or organization actively looking to acquire the registration of a domain name through a financial transaction.
Chapter: 3, 10, 11, 12, 13

ccTLDs: Country code top-level domains are those which are assigned for a specific country or region, such as CO.UK for the United Kingdom, .CA for Canada, .FR for France, and so on.
Chapter: 1, 3, 21

Cease & desist letter: A type of legal recourse in which a company issues a letter to another party warning them to end the offending action or else more severe legal actions will be taken.
Chapter: 10, 14

CIO: Chief Information Officer role at a corporation who is typically in charge of managing the company's IT resources and strategy. As such, they may be involved in decisions regarding a digital asset like domain names.
Chapter: 15

CISO: Chief Information Security Officer role at a corporation who is typically responsible for an organization's cybersecurity, which includes intellectual property like domain names.
Chapter: 15

Corporation Service Company (CSC): Brand protection agency with over 100 years experience of assisting major brands in protecting their IP and trademark.
Chapter: 3, 5, 6, 10, 16

Cybercriminal: A class of bad actors who specifically use the internet to conduct illegal activity, including hacking into systems, impersonating brands/companies to conduct scams, stealing IP and data, using ransomware, identity theft, and even stealing domain names.
Chapter: 1, 6, 11, 12, 14, 18, 20

Cybersquatting: The act of purposefully registering a domain name associated with a known entity or IP in the hopes of profiting from doing so, especially by less-than-ethical means. For instance, buying the name of a celebrity or competing brand and then placing ad space on the site to profit from the web traffic—or even trying to hold the domain name for "ransom" and extort the known entity.
Chapter: 2, 6, 14, 16

DKIM: Stands for DomainKeys identified Mail, which is a protocol for email identification using cryptography to verify the authenticity of an email.
Chapter: 20

DMARC: Domain-based Message Authentication, Reporting, and Conformance is a protocol for email authentication designed to protect email users from cybersecurity threats. Domain owners use DMARC to determine what should happen if an incoming email fails the authentication process and to identify other threats related to the email server.
Chapter: 20

DNS server: The Domain Name System server is a type of machine used to translate a domain name into an IP address, which allows for users to access the intended website.
Chapter: 20

Domain agreement: A legal agreement between two parties—typically the seller and the buyer—about the terms of transferring a domain name registration from one to the other.
Chapter: 11

Domain name: An indefinite lived, intangible digital asset used to identify your company or brand, especially as your online address. As an asset class, they are also counted as intellectual property (IP). While not all domain names have a dedicated website, a website with the right domain name will experience increased traffic.
Chapter: 1

Domain name auctions: Live or online, these open market events are dedicated to selling a domain name to the highest bidder.
Chapter: 3, 4, 11, 15, 16, 17, 18

Domain name attorneys: Class of IP attorney who specializes in domain name assets.
Chapter: 17, 18

Domain name financing: A financing agreement in which the buyer gets access to the domain name registration in exchange for paying installments spelled out in specific terms. Domain names may be financed directly with an owner, through a financial institution, or through being backed by investors.
Chapter: 3, 12, 13, 18

Domain name marketplace: A marketplace specifically designated for domain transactions, such as Sedo, the first online marketplace established in 2001, though GoDaddy now operates the largest marketplace in the industry.
Chapter: 9, 17

Dropcatching: The practice of buying a domain name when the registrant fails to renew the registration.
Chapter: 10, 11

Dropcatch services: Services that equip investors in acquiring domain names of interest within milliseconds of the name becoming available.
Chapter: 10, 11

Drop services: Services that enable parties to monitor a name that is about to become available and bid on the acquisition within milliseconds of the registration dropping.
Chapter: 4

E-commerce transaction services: Any service that provides transaction capabilities for a brand, such as Shopify, Stripe, or Square.
Chapter: 3

Escrow.com: The go-to escrow service for domain name transactions. In financed transactions, they serve as an intermediary between the two parties, holding the registration in the event the

purchaser defaults and the domain name needs to be returned to the seller.
Chapter: 11, 17, 18, 20

Exact match domain (EMD): When the SLD is an exact match for your brand or product's name. For instance, FBI.gov for the Federal Bureau of Investigation, or AirJordan.com for the Air Jordan line of shoes.
Chapter: 3, 4, 8, 21, 22

Errors & Omissions (E&O) insurance: A special rider for business insurance that protects the company in the event of an unintentional trademark or IP infringement.
Chapter: 10

General Data Protection Regulation (GDPR): An international law enacted by the European Union in 2018 to protect the privacy of domain name owners within the EU. However, the nature of the regulation and internationality of the internet essentially means the regulations apply worldwide.
Chapter: 6

gTLDs: Generic top-level domains are the most popular and recognizable extensions on the market, and therefore, also the most valuable.
Chapter: 1

ICANN: Internet Corporation for Assigned Names and Numbers, a nonprofit, international partnership that was established in 1998. Based in Los Angeles, their purpose is to develop and enforce policies for unique identifiers on the internet, including which TLDs may be used. They also established the Uniform Domain Name Resolution Policy in 1999.
Chapter: 1, 2, 3, 6, 14, 21

Investors: Individuals or organizations that acquire domain names as an investment strategy, often "flipping" the names by reselling them after their value has increased.
Chapter: 1, 3, 4, 5, 11, 13, 15, 17

Intellectual property (IP): Any work or invention belonging to a company that resulted from their creative work. IP is usually closely identified with the company's brand or trademarks. Ex: *Star Wars* and all its related properties make up the intellectual property of LucasFilm. Likewise, the domain name you created (or acquired) is your intellectual property. Some IP, like domain names, quality as indefinite-lived, intangible assets.
Chapter: 3, 4, 5, 6, 7, 10, 15, 17

IP address: Internet Protocol is a set of rules that assigns a numeric-based identifier that is assigned to every device (computer, smartphone, tablet, etc.) that is connected to a computer network. The IP address appears as a series of numbers that holds the location information for the connected devices.
Chapter: 20

IP lawyers: Attorneys who are knowledgeable and experienced in laws concerning intellectual property. This can include domain names as well as trademarks.
Chapter: 3, 6

Keyword domains: A domain name that is based on a searchable keyword rather than the name of a company. For example, cookie delivery company Tiff's Treats uses the keyword domain "CookieDelivery.com." However, since the Panda (2011) and Penguin (2012) updates on Google, keyword domains no longer wield the same SEO power they once held.
Chapter: 1, 8, 9

KYC procedures: "Know Your Customer" procedures, which refers to an ID verification process designed to ensure the identity of the individual you're conducting business with. It's a due diligence process intended to prevent fraud or other financial crimes.
Chapter: 17

No-compete clause: In a domain name transaction, it's normal for a corporate seller to insist the buyer of the domain name will not use it in direct competition with the seller.
Chapter: 15

OFAC (Office of Foreign Assets Control): An office of the US Treasury Department that oversees international transactions, including any restrictions related to foreign policy or national security.
Chapter: 17

Parked pages: When a domain name is registered but is not being actively used. That is, the domain name has no associated website or service to be accessed. Often, they are being held by the registrant for future use. Chapter: 2

Parking services: Services who assist individuals or brands with any parked domain names which can provide a small income stream.
Chapter: 3

Registrant: The individual or company who owns the registration of a domain name. For simplicity, we often refer to them as "the owner," though technically, the registrar always holds ownership of the actual domain name.
Chapter: 2, 3, 5, 6, 9, 11, 15, 16, 17, 18

Registrars: Companies that sell domain names, often focusing on a select group of TLDs.
Chapter: 1, 2, 3, 4, 6, 10, 17, 18, 19, 21

Registry: A company that owns, operates, and maintains a TLD. For instance, Verisign is the owner of all .COM and .NET top-level domains. They are the owner of the TLD but make money by allowing registrars to issue registrations for the names.
Chapter: 1, 3, 4

Second-Level Domains (SLDs): The part of the domain name to the left side of the dot. Most often, it is the name of the company that owns it, such as Google.
Chapter: 1, 8, 9, 10, 12, 15, 16, 18, 22

SEO (Search Engine Optimization): Marketing term referring to how easy it is to find your company/brand online. TLDs and SLDs can both factor into how optimal your domain name is for a search engine, and therefore, how easy it is for customers to find you.
Chapter: 1, 8, 9, 18, 21, 22

SMTP (Simple Mail Transfer Protocol): A standard communication protocol for email used by mail servers and other digital messaging applications.
Chapter: 20

Speculators: Individuals or businesses that identify, register, and acquire generic domain names as an investment strategy, especially in "flipping" them, similar to real estate.
Chapter: 1, 3, 5, 6

SPF (Sender Policy Framework): A standard for email authentication that domain owners can use to specify their email server(s). For the purpose of cybersecurity, SPFs also make it more difficult for a bad actor to commit fraud like identity spoofing.
Chapter: 20

SSL certificate: Secure Sockets Layer certificates are a type of security file hosted on a website's server and enables the website to use a HTTPS address, which is more secure than HTTP.
Chapter: 20

sTLDs: Sponsored top-level domains are common ones which have restrictions around their use, such as .GOV, .EDU, and .MIL.
Chapter: 1

Top-Level Domains (TLDs): The part of the domain name to the right of the dot. The most common include .COM, .NET, and .ORG.
Chapter: 1, 2, 8, 9, 10, 21, 22

Trademark: A form of official legal protection for specific types of IP, such as brand names, phrases, or logos. Ex: Taylor Swift has trademarked her name and even some of her lyrics to protect them from abuse and misuse.
Chapter: 6, 7, 8, 10, 11, 12, 14, 15, 17, 19, 22

TXT records: A DNS TXT record can be used to help verify who owns the domain name.
Chapter: 20

Uniform Domain Name Dispute Resolution Policy (UDRP or UDNRP): A process developed by ICANN that allows legitimate domain name owners to go after bad actors who have stolen a domain name, committed cybersquatting, or other illegal activity related to their domain name.
Chapter: 6, 14, 19

Usenet names: The oldest set of domain names, largely used by universities for internal communications.
Chapter: 2

US Patent and Trademark Office: The agency tasked with authorizing and granting legal protection to patents and trademarks in the United States.
Chapter: 6, 10

Valuation tools: Online resource designed to give potential domain name buyers with an estimated value of domain names they are interested in. Unfortunately, they are not very accurate.
Chapter: 5, 8, 15

Wayback machine: A tool created by Archive.org which allows users to look up old web pages.
Chapter: 6

Web Hosting Provider: A company that provides hosting services for a brand's website, such as GoDaddy, Wordpress, Squarespace, or Wix.
Chapter: 3

WHOIS database: Any online database that allows users to search for the owner of a domain name or the history of registration for a domain name.
Chapter: 6, 11, 17

Wildcard certificate: A digital certificate designed for use with multiple subdomains.
Chapter: 20

WIPO: The World Intellectual Property Organization, which helps oversee and set out guidelines and regulations for domain name legal cases.
Chapter: 17

XML sitemap: XML stands for Extensible Markup Language, and the XML sitemap is a file that provides information about every page on a specific website.

Chapter: 20

RESOURCES

List of the Top 150 Most Expensive Domain Names:
www.brannans.com/news-resources/
the-top-150-most-expensive-domain-names/

Domain News and Media
www.brannans.com/news-resources/

Contact Brannans
https://www.brannans.com/contact/

Trademark Search tool:
https://tmsearch.uspto.gov/search/search-information

ENDNOTES

1   Gladwell, Malcolm. *Outliers: The Story of Success.* New York: Little, Brown and Company, 2008.

2   Ericsson, Anders, Ralf Th. Krampe, and Clemens Tesch-Römer. "The Role of Deliberate Practice in the Acquisition of Expert Performance." *Psychological Review* 100, no. 3 (1993): 363-406.

3   Ghayas, Adnan. "What Are Digital and Analog Mobile Networks?" Commsbrief. November 17, 2019. https://commsbrief.com/difference-between-digital-and-analogue-mobile-networks/.

4   Hunt, Rockwell D. California's Stately Hall of Fame. Stockton, California: The College of the Pacific (1950), 237–242.

5   It should be noted that even though many UK-based brands have tried to make the switch to simply using .UK, you can't change decades of consumer behavior so quickly. The .CO.UK ccTLD is still preferred over the shorter .UK extension, and perhaps it will always be this way.

6   ICANN. "What Does ICANN Do?" Icann.org. Accessed January 31, 2024. https://www.icann.org/resources/pages/what-2012-02-25-en.

7   Murphy, Kevin. "O.co Loses 61% of Its Traffic to O.com." Domain Incite. March 3, 2012. https://domainincite.com/7992-o-co-loses-61-of-its-traffic-to-o-com.

8   If you don't have the exact match .COM TLD for your brand but you'd like to discuss with our team at Brannan's, please reach out to learn more about how we can help you.

9   Allemann, Andrew. "SEC Filing Shows Hefty Price for .Club and .Design." DomainNameWire.com. August 9, 2021. https://domainnamewire.com/2021/08/09/sec-filing-shows-hefty-price-for-club-and-design/.

10   Brannans. "The Top 150 Most Expensive Domain Names." Brannans.com. https://www.brannans.com/news-resources/the-top-150-most-expensive-domain-names/.

11   Allemann, Andrew. "To the Moon! Rocket Mortgage pays $14M+ for Rocket.com Domain Name." DomainNameWire.com. October 28, 2024. https://domainnamewire.com/2024/10/28/to-the-moon-rocket-mortgage-pays-14m-for-rocket-com-domain-name/

12   Allemann, Andrew. "Kevin Ham Sells Domain Names to GoDaddy." DomainNameWire.com. October 25, 2017. https://domainnamewire.com/2017/10/25/kevin-ham-sells-domain-names-godaddy/.

13   Alleman, Andrew. "GoDaddy Paid 50 Million for Two Latest Domain Portfolio Acquisitions." DomainNameWire.com. November 8, 2017. https://domainnamewire.com/2017/11/08/godaddy-paid-50-million-two-latest-domain-portfolio-acquisitions/

14   GoDaddy. "Why Buy a Domain with GoDaddy." GoDaddy.com. Accessed September 4, 2024. https://www.godaddy.com/domains.

15   NTLD Stats. "Registrar Overview." nTLDStats.com. Accessed September 4, 2024. https://ntldstats.com/registrar.

16   Allemann, Andrew. "Directnic Acquires Domain Name Registrar Fabulous.com." DomainNameWire.com. October 31, 2017, https://domainnamewire.com/2017/10/31/directnic-acquires-domain-name-registrar-fabulous-com/.

17   ICANN Wiki. "Ron Jackson." ICANNWiki.org. Accessed March 4, 2024. https://icannwiki.org/index.php?title=Ron_Jackson.

18   NameBio. Accessed March 4, 2024. https://namebio.com/.

19   Lindenthal, Thies. "Valuable Words: The Price Dynamics of Internet Domain Names." *Journal of the Association for Information Science and Technology*, (May 2014), DOI: 10.1002/asi.

20   Escrow.com. "Alternative Investing: A Comparison Between Traditional Instruments and Web Domains." (2018), 14.

21   Ibid, 5.

22   Ibid, 7.

23   Ibid, 9.

24   Allemann, Andrew Allemann. "How Dropbox Got the Dropbox.com Domain Name." DomainNameWire.com. September 19, 2018. https://domainnamewire.com/2018/09/19/dropbox-domain-name/.

25   SEC Archives. Accessed March 7, 2024. https://www.sec.gov/Archives/edgar/data/1116521/000119312511336630/R13.htm#.

26   Howard, Ben. "The Top 10 Most Expensive Domains Ever Sold."
      Name.com. December 20, 2022. https://www.name.com/blog/
      the-top-10-most-expensive-domains-ever-sold.

27   Wolinsky, Jacob. "Churn Rate for Domains Is Over 30 Percent
      According to a New Study." ValueWalk.com. September 25, 2023.
      https://www.valuewalk.com/churn-rate-for-domains/.

28   Kaufman, Wendy. "Verizon Wins 'Cybersquatting' Lawsuit." NPR.
      org. December 25, 2008. https://www.npr.org/templates/story/
      story.php?storyId=98706077#.

29   Allemann, Andrew. "Verizon Wins $450k Cybersquatting
      Judgment." DomainNameWire.com. January 5,
      2024. https://domainnamewire.com/2024/01/05/
      verizon-wins-450k-cybersquatting-judgment.

30   Iles, James. "Brent Oxley Loses Access to Create.com, Plus
      Millions of Dollars Worth of His Domains." JamesNames.com.
      March 4, 2021. https://jamesnames.com/2021/03/brent-oxley/#.

31   City of Las Vegas. "Strong Growth For Tourism." LasVegasNevada.
      gov. May 4, 2023. https://www.lasvegasnevada.gov/News/Blog/
      Detail/strong-growth-for-tourism.

32   Silver, Elliot Silver. "Report: LasVegas.com Deal
      Valued at Nearly $90 Million." DomainInvesting.
      com. November 6, 2015. https://domaininvesting.com/
      report-lasvegas-com-would-be-largest-domain-sale/.

33   LasVegas.com. Home page. Accessed March 29, 2024. https://
      lasvegas.com.

34   CHESS.com. "Chess.com Reaches 100 Million Members!" Chess. com. December 16, 2022. https://www.chess.com/article/view/ chesscom-reaches-100-million-members.

35   Holland, Taylor. "What Is Branding? A Brief History." Skyword.com. August 11, 2017. https://www.skyword.com/ contentstandard/branding-brief-history/.

36   Quinn, James. "Amazon's Jeff Bezos: With Jeremy Clarkson, We're Entering a New Golden Age of Television." *The Telegraph*. August 16, 2015. https://www.telegraph.co.uk/technology/ amazon/11800890/jeff-bezos-interview-amazon-prime-jeremy-clarkson.html.

37   Miller, Carly. "9 Huge Branding Fails From Famous Companies." TailorBrands. Accessed March 29, 2024. https://www.tailorbrands. com/blog/9-huge-branding-fails-from-your-favorite-companies.

38   Ogg, Erica. "The Beatles Come to iTunes at Last." CNet. com. November 16, 2010. https://www.cnet.com/culture/ the-beatles-come-to-itunes-at-last/.

39   Tiff's Treats. "Our Story." TiffsTreats.com. Accessed April 1, 2024. https://www.cookiedelivery.com/about/our-story.aspx.

40   Zournas, Konstantinos. "The Domain Name Purple.Com Was Sold For $900,000." OnlineDomain.com. March 17, 2018. https://onlinedomain.com/2018/03/17/domain-name-news/ the-domain-name-purple-com-was-sold-for-900000/.

41   Iles, James. "Case Study: Why Did Purple Upgrade to Purple.com for $900,000 When It Did?" JamesNames.com. March 8, 2021. https://jamesnames.com/2021/03/case-study-why-did-purple-upgrade-to-purple-com-for-900000-when-it-did/.

42   Silver, Eliot. "KHY.com Acquired by Kylie Jenner."
      DomainInvesting.com. October 25, 2023. https://domaininvesting.
      com/khy-com-acquired-by-kylie-jenner/.

43   Beveridge, Charles E. "Frederick Law Olmstead Sr." Olmstead.org.
      June 22, 2023. https://olmsted.org/frederick-law-olmsted-sr/.

44   Library of Congress. "Parks for the People: Frederick Law
      Olmstead and the Evolution of the Olmstead Firm, 1822-1900."
      LOC.gov. Accessed April 8, 2024. https://www.loc.gov/collections/
      olmsted-associates-records/articles-and-essays/timelines/
      evolution-of-olmsted-firm-1822-to-1900/.

45   Kang, Tricia. "160 Years of Central Park: A Brief History." Central
      Park Conservancy. June 1, 2017. Accessed April 8, 2024. https://
      www.centralparknyc.org/articles/central-park-history.

46   Fonrouge, Gabrielle. "Overstock.com Will Change Website Name
      to Bed Bath & Beyond as Deal Closes." CNBC. June 28, 2023.
      https://www.cnbc.com/2023/06/28/overstockcom-to-rename-
      website-bed-bath-beyond.html.

47   Townsend, Lawrence G., Intellectual Property Lawyer. "Michael
      Jackson Estate Objects to KingOfPop.com to Sell Popcorn."
      LGT-Law.com. August 6, 2019. https://www.lgt-law.com/
      blog/2019/08/michael-jackson-estate-objects-to-kingofpopcom-
      to-sell-popcorn/.

48   Allemann, Andrew. "Michael Jackson Estate Gets
      KingOfPop.com Domain Name." DomainNameWire.com.
      July 8, 2019. https://domainnamewire.com/2019/07/08/
      michael-jackson-estate-gets-kingofpop-com-domain-name/.

49   Trademark Search tool can be found at https://tmsearch.uspto.gov/search/search-information

50   Silver, Elliot. "Honeymoons.Com: Domain Name Led to 10x Revenue." DomainInvesting.com. January 10, 2024. https://domaininvesting.com/honeymoons-com-domain-name-led-to-10x-revenue/.

51   Frida Baby. "LinkedIn Company Page: About." Accessed September 4, 2024. https://www.linkedin.com/company/fridababy/.

52   Muscovitch, Zak. "A Short History of Cybersquatting Law." DNAttorney.com. Accessed April 9, 2024. https://dnattorney.com/a-short-history-of-cybersquatting-law/.

53   Nolo. "Cybersquatting: What It Is and What Can Be Done About It." Nolo.com. Accessed April 9, 2024. https://www.nolo.com/legal-encyclopedia/cybersquatting-what-what-can-be-29778.html.

54   Carnegie, Dale. *How to Win Friends and Influence People*, (New York: Simon & Schuster, 1936), 108.

55   Website URL, https://www.brannans.com/news-resources/the-top-150-most-expensive-domain-names/

56   Allemann, Andrew., "Judge Orders Nissan.com Transferred Back to Estate of Uzi Nissan." DomainNameWire.com. April 17, 2024. https://domainnamewire.com/2024/04/17/judge-orders-nissan-com-transferred-back-to-estate-of-uzi-nissan/.

57   You may consult the glossary for definitions for many of the technical terms listed here.

58   For more information, see: https://support.google.com/a/
      answer/7009324?hl=en

59   ICANN = The Internet Corporation for Assigned Names and
      Numbers, a regulatory nonprofit established in 1998 to set
      international standards for the internet, including administration
      rules for domain names. The organization is overseen by a board
      of sixteen members, including the CEO.

60   New York Film Academy. "How RED Cameras Changed the
      Game." NYFA.edu. August 7, 2015. https://www.nyfa.edu/
      student-resources/how-red-cameras-changed-the-game/.

61   Graham, Jefferson. "How Ring's Founder Created
      A Doorbell Worth $1 Billion To Amazon." Investors.
      com. October 11, 2021. https://www.investors.
      com/news/management/leaders-and-success/
      jamie-siminoff-created-a-doorbell-worth-1-billion-to-amazon/.

62   Kharpal, Arjun. "Man Buys Google.com for $12 for 1 Minute,
      Gets Reward." CNBC.com. October 13, 2015. https://www.cnbc.
      com/2015/10/13/man-buys-google-domain-for-12-dollars-for-1-
      minute-gets-reward-gives-to-charity.html.

63   Silver, Elliot. "Gold.com Appears to Have Been Sold."
      DomainInvesting.com. December 30, 2019. https://
      domaininvesting.com/gold-com-appears-sold/.

64   Stankova, Monica. "JM Bullion Acquires Gold.com, Joining
      Silver.com in Its Prestigious Domain Portfolio." SmartBranding.
      com. Accessed May 24, 2024. https://smartbranding.com/
      jm-bullion-acquires-gold-com-joining-silver-com-in-its-
      prestigious-domain-portfolio/.

65   CNET. "Vodka.com Domain Sells for $3 million." CNET.com.
      January 14, 2007. https://www.cnet.com/tech/tech-industry/
      vodka-com-domain-sells-for-3-million/.

66   Carlson, Nicholas. "How Twitter.com Went From a $7,500
      Domain To A $1 Billion Company." Business Insider. September 14,
      2010. https://www.businessinsider.com/how-twittercom-went-
      from-a-7500-domain-to-a-1-billion-company-2010-9.

67   HypeBeast. "Elon Musk Has Bought Back His Old X.com Domain
      From PayPal," HypeBeast.com. July 2017, accessed May 24, 2024.
      https://hypebeast.com/2017/7/elon-musk-x-com-domain-paypal.

68   Allemann, Andrew. "Ice.com, a Domain with a Rich History,
      Sells Again. This Time for $3.5 million." DomainNameWire.
      com. July 17, 2018. https://domainnamewire.com/2018/07/17/
      ice-com-a-domain-with-a-rich-history-sells-again-this-time-
      for-3-5-million/.

69   Iles, James. "Case Study: Why Musk Acquired Tesla.
      com for $11 Million." JamesNames.com. August
      6, 2021. https://jamesnames.com/2021/08/
      case-study-why-musk-acquired-tesla-com-for-11-million/.

70   Kincaid, Jason. "Dropbox Acquires The Domain Everyone
      Thought It Had: Dropbox.com." TechCrunch.com. October 13,
      2009. https://techcrunch.com/2009/10/13/dropbox-acquires-the-
      domain-everyone-thought-it-had-dropbox-com/.

71   Allemann, Andrew. "Did Zoom pay $2 million
      for Zoom.com?" DomainNameWire.com. March
      23, 2019. https://domainnamewire.com/2019/03/23/
      did-zoom-pay-2-million-for-zoom-com/.

72   Vio. "FindHotel Is Now Vio.com." Medium.com.
       December 8, 2022. https://medium.com/viodotcom/
       findhotel-is-now-vio-com-154c4b9da045.

73   Kharpal, Arjun. "Google Buys Domain
       abcdefghijklmnopqrstuvwxyz.com." CNBC.com. October 8, 2015.
       https://www.cnbc.com/2015/10/08/google-buys-alphabet-
       domain-name-abcdefghijklmnopqrstuvwxyzcom.html.

74   Campbell, Colin. *Start. Scale. Exit. Repeat.* (Charleston: Forbes
       Books, 2023), 58.

75   Mason, James. "Pink.com Acquired by Mark
       Monitor on Behalf of L Brands." JamesNames.com.
       November 6, 2020. https://jamesnames.com/2020/11/
       pink-com-acquired-by-markmonitor-on-behalf-of-l-brands/

76   Idealab. "Home Page." Idealab.com. Accessed May 24, 2024.
       https://www.idealab.com/.